POLITICALLY INCORRECT
FOR EVERY OCCASION
AND SOME YOU SHOULD
PROBABLY NEVER TELL

BY JAMES HERSHEY JR

A husband and wife are trying to set up a new password for their computer. The husband puts, "My penis," and the wife falls on the ground laughing because on the screen it says, "Error. Not long enough."

Wife: "How would you describe me?"
Husband: "ABCDEFGHIJK."
Wife: "What does that mean?"
Husband: "Adorable, beautiful, cute, delightful, elegant, fashionable, gorgeous, and hot."
Wife: "Aw, thank you, but what about IJK?"
Husband: "I'm just kidding!"

The teacher asked Jimmy, "Why is your cat at school today Jimmy?" Jimmy replied crying, "Because I heard my daddy tell my mommy, 'I am going to eat that pussy once Jimmy leaves for school today!'"

Teacher: "Kids, what does the chicken give you?"
Student: "Meat!"
Teacher: "Very good! Now what does the pig give you?"
Student: "Bacon!"
Teacher: "Great! And what does the fat cow give you?"
Student: "Homework!"

Yo momma is so fat, I took a picture of her last Christmas and it's still printing.

A mother is in the kitchen making dinner for her family when her daughter walks in. "Mother, where do babies come from?" The mother thinks for a few seconds and says, "Well dear, Mommy and Daddy fall in love and get married. One night they go into their bedroom, they kiss and hug, and have sex." The daughter looks puzzled so the mother continues, "That means the daddy puts his penis in the mommy's vagina. That's how you get a baby, honey." The child seems to comprehend. "Oh, I see, but the other night when I came into your room you had daddy's penis in your mouth. What do you get when you do that?" "Jewelry, my dear. Jewelry."

Yo momma is so fat when she got on the scale it said, "I need your weight not your phone number."

A family is at the dinner table. The son asks the father, "Dad, how many kinds of boobs are there?" The father, surprised, answers, "Well, son, a woman goes through three phases. In her 20s, a woman's breasts are like melons, round and firm. In her 30s and 40s, they are like pears, still nice, hanging a bit. After 50, they are like onions." "Onions?" the son asks. "Yes. You see them and they make you cry." This infuriated his wife and daughter. The daughter asks, "Mom, how many different kinds of willies are there?" The mother smiles and says, "Well, dear, a man goes through three phases also. In his 20s, his willy is like an oak tree, mighty and hard. In his 30s and 40s, it's like a birch, flexible but reliable. After his 50s, it's like a Christmas tree." "A Christmas tree?" the daughter asks. "Yes, dead from the root up and the balls are just for decoration."

A child asked his father, "How were people born?" So his father said, "Adam and Eve made babies, then their babies became adults and made babies, and so on." The child then went to his mother, asked her the same question and she told him, "We were monkeys then we evolved to become like we are now." The child ran back to his father and said, "You lied to me!" His father replied, "No, your mom was talking about her side of the family."

On the roof of a very tall building are four men; one is Asian, one is Mexican, one is black, and the last one is white. The Asian walks to the ledge and says, "This is for all my people" and jumps off the roof. Next, the Mexican walks to the ledge and also says, "This is for all my people" and then he jumps off the roof. Next is the black guy's turn. The black guy walks to the ledge and says, "This is for all my people" and then throws the white guy off the roof.

Yo momma is so fat that when she went to the beach a whale swam up and sang, "We are family, even though you're fatter than me."

Yo mamma is so ugly when she tried to join an ugly contest they said, "Sorry, no professionals."

A blonde, a redhead, and a brunette were all lost in the desert. They found a lamp and rubbed it. A genie popped out and granted them each one wish. The redhead wished to be back home. Poof! She was back home. The brunette wished to be at home with her family. Poof! She was back home with her family. The blonde said, "Awwww, I wish my friends were here."

What did God say when he made the first black man? "Damn, I burnt one."

Yo momma's so fat and old when God said, "Let there be light," he asked your mother to move out of the way.

Blonde: "What does IDK stand for?"
Brunette: "I don't know."
Blonde: "OMG, nobody does!"

What did one saggy boob say to the other saggy boob? "We better get some support before someone thinks we're nuts!"

Wife: "I look fat. Can you give me a compliment?"
Husband: "You have perfect eyesight."

Two blondes fell down a hole. One said, "Its dark in here isn't it?" The other replied, "I don't know; I can't see."

Do not be racist; be like Mario. He's an Italian plumber, who was made by the Japanese, speaks English, looks like a Mexican, jumps like a black man, and grabs coins like a Jew!

There was a blonde, a redhead, and a brunette. They were all trapped on an island and the nearest shore was 50 miles away. The redhead swam trying to make it to the other shore she swam 15 miles, drowned, and died. The brunette swam 24 miles, drowned, and died. The blonde swam 25 miles, got tired, and swam back.

Q: Why can't a blonde dial 911?
A: She can't find the eleven.

What happens to a frog's car when it breaks down?
It gets toad away

A teacher is teaching a class and she sees that Johnny isn't paying attention, so she asks him, "If there are three ducks sitting on a fence, and you shoot one, how many are left?" Johnny says, "None." The teacher asks, "Why?" Johnny says, "Because the shot scared them all off." The teacher says, "No, two, but I like how you're thinking." Johnny asks the teacher, "If you see three women walking out of an ice cream parlor, one is licking her ice cream, one is sucking her ice cream, and one is biting her ice cream, which one is married?" The teacher says, "The one sucking her ice cream." Johnny says, "No, the one with the wedding ring, but I like how you're thinking!"

As an airplane is about to crash, a female passenger jumps up frantically and announces, "If I'm going to die, I want to die feeling like a woman." She removes all her clothing and asks, "Is there someone on this plane who is man enough to make me feel like a woman?" A man stands up, removes his shirt and says, "Here, iron this!"

How do you blindfold a Chinese person? Put floss over their eyes.

A little girl and boy are fighting about the differences between the sexes, and which one is better. Finally, the boy drops his pants and says, "Here's something I have that you'll never have!" The little girl is pretty upset by this, since it is clearly true, and runs home crying. A while later, she comes running back with a smile on her face. She drops her pants and says, "My mommy says that with one of these, I can have as many of those as I want!"

Your momma is so ugly she made One Direction go another direction.

A teacher wanted to teach her students about self-esteem, so she asked anyone who thought they were stupid to stand up. One kid stood up and the teacher was surprised. She didn't think anyone would stand up so she asked him, "Why did you stand up?" He answered, "I didn't want to leave you standing up by yourself."

A man kills a deer and takes it home to cook for dinner. Both he and his wife decide that they won't tell the kids what kind of meat it is, but will give them a clue and let them guess. The dad said, "Well it's what Mommy calls me sometimes." The little girl screamed to her brother, "Don't eat it. It's an asshole!

Yo momma's so stupid; she put two quarters in her ears and thought she was listening to 50 Cent.

A guy took his blonde girlfriend to her first football game. They had great seats right behind their team's bench. After the game, he asked her how she liked the experience. "Oh, I really liked it," she replied, "especially the tight pants and all the big muscles, but I just couldn't understand why they were killing each other over 25 cents." Dumbfounded, her date asked, "What do you mean?" "Well, they flipped a coin, one team got it, and then for the rest of the game, all they kept screaming was, 'Get the quarterback! Get the quarterback!' I'm like, hello? It's only 25 cents!"

A black boy walks into the kitchen where his mother is baking and accidentally pulls the flour over onto his head. He turns to his mother and says, "Look Mama, I'm a white boy!" His mother smacks him and says, "Go tell your Daddy what you just said!" The boy finds his father and says, "Look Daddy, I'm a white boy!" His Daddy bends him over, spanks him, stands the boy back up, and says, "Now, what do you have to say for yourself?" The boy replies, "I've only been a white boy for five minutes and I already hate you black people!"

Having sex is like playing bridge. If you don't have a good partner, you'd better have a good hand.

A black Jewish boy runs home from school one day and asks his father, "Daddy, am I more Jewish or more black?" The dad replies, "Why do you want to know, son?" "Because a kid at school is selling a bike for $50 and I want to know if I should talk him down to $40 or just steal it!"

A man and woman had been married for 30 years, and in those 30 years, they always left the lights off when having sex. He was embarrassed and scared that he couldn't please her, so he always used a big dildo on her. All these years she had no clue. One day, she decided to reach over and flip the light switch on and saw that he was using a dildo. She said "I knew it, asshole, explain the dildo!" He said, "Explain the kids!"

Q: What did the duck say when he bought lipstick?
A: "Put it on my bill."

Q: Why do Mexicans eat beans for dinner?
A: So they can take bubble baths.

A few months after his parents were divorced, little Johnny passed by his mom's bedroom and saw her rubbing her body and moaning, "I need a man, I need a man!" Over the next couple of months, he saw her doing this several times. One day, he came home from school and heard her moaning. When he peeked into her bedroom, he saw a man on top of her. Little Johnny ran into his room, took off his clothes, threw himself on his bed, started stroking himself, and moaning, "Oh, I need a bike! I need a bike!"

Yo momma is so fat her bellybutton gets home 15 minutes before she does.

Why do women make better soldiers? Because they can bleed for a week and not die.

A boy says to a girl, "So, sex at my place?" "Yeah!" "Okay, but I sleep in a bunk bed with my younger brother, and he thinks we're making sandwiches, so we have to have a code. Cheese means faster and tomato means harder, okay?" Later on the girl is yelling, "Cheese cheese, tomato tomato!" The younger brother says, "Stop making sandwiches! You're getting mayo all over my bed!"

Yo momma's so fat, that when she fell, no one was laughing but the ground was cracking up.

Q: How do Chinese people name their babies?
A: They throw them down the stairs to see what noise they make.

Whenever your ex says, "You'll never find someone like me," the answer to that is, "That's the point."

Maria went home happy, telling her mother about how she earned $20 by climbing a tree. Her mom responded, "Maria, they just wanted to see your panties!" Maria replied, "See Mom, I was smart, I took them off!"

A robber comes into the store & steals a TV. A blonde runs after him and says, "Wait, you forgot the remote!"

Yo momma is so fat that Dora can't even explore her!

A bride tells her husband, "Honey, you know I'm a virgin and I don't know anything about sex. Can you explain it to me first?" "Okay, sweetheart. Putting it simply, we will call your private place 'the prison' and call my private thing 'the prisoner'. So what we do is put the prisoner in the prison." And they made love for the first time and the husband was smiling with satisfaction. Nudging him, his bride giggles, "Honey the prisoner seems to have escaped." Turning on his side, he smiles and says, "Then we will have to re-imprison him." After the second time, the bride says, "Honey, the prisoner is out again!" The husband rises to the occasion and they made love again. The bride again says, "Honey, the prisoner escaped again," to which the husband yelled, "Hey, it's not a life sentence!!!"

Why did I get divorced? Well, last week was my birthday. My wife didn't wish me a happy birthday. My parents forgot and so did my kids. I went to work and even my colleagues didn't wish me a happy birthday. As I entered my office, my secretary said, "Happy birthday, boss!" I felt so special. She asked me out for lunch. After lunch, she invited me to her apartment. We went there and she said, "Do you mind if I go into the bedroom for a minute?" "Okay," I said. She came out 5 minutes later with a birthday cake, my wife, my parents, my kids, my friends, & my colleagues all yelling, "SURPRISE!!!" while I was waiting on the sofa... naked.

Reaching the end of a job interview, the Human Resources Officer asks a young engineer fresh out of the Massachusetts Institute of Technology, "And what starting salary are you looking for?" The engineer replies, "In the region of $125,000 a year, depending on the benefits package." The interviewer inquires, "Well, what would you say to a package of five weeks vacation, 14 paid holidays, full medical and dental, company matching retirement fund to 50% of salary, and a company car leased every two years, say, a red Corvette?" The engineer sits up straight and says, "Wow! Are you kidding?" The interviewer replies, "Yeah, but you started it."

Yo momma's so fat she needs cheat codes for Wii Fit.

Yo momma is so stupid she brought a spoon to the super bowl.

A man was having premature ejaculation problems so he went to the doctor. The doctor said, "When you feel like you are getting ready to ejaculate, try startling yourself." That same day the man went to the store and bought himself a starter pistol and ran home to his wife. That night the two were having sex and found themselves in the 69 position. The man felt the urge to ejaculate and fired the starter pistol. The next day he went back to the doctor who asked how it went. The man answered, "Not well. When I fired the pistol, my wife pooped on my face, bit three inches off my penis, and my neighbor came out of the closet with his hands in the air."

10 Facts About You:
1. You're reading this now.
2. You're realizing that this is a stupid fact.

4. You didn't notice I skipped number 3.
5. You're checking now.
6. You're smiling.
7. You're still reading this even though it is stupid.
9. You didn't realize I skipped number 8.
10. You're checking again and smiling because you fell for it again.
11. You're enjoying this.
12. You didn't realize I said 10 facts not 12.

Yo momma is so stupid she climbed over a glass wall to see what was on the other side.

There was a blonde who just got sick and tired of all the blonde jokes. One evening, she went home and memorized all the state capitals. Back in the office the next day, some guy started telling a dumb blonde joke. She interrupted him with a shrill announcement, "I've had it up to here with these blonde jokes. I want you to know that this blonde went home last night and did something probably none of you could do. I memorized all the state capitals." One of the guys, of course, said, "I don't believe you. What is the capital of Nevada?" "N," she answered.

Sarah goes to school, and the teacher says, "Today we are going to learn multi-syllable words, class. Does anybody have an example of a multi-syllable word?" Sarah waves her hand, "Me, Miss Rogers, me, me!" Miss Rogers says, "All right, Sarah, what is your multi-syllable word?" Sarah says, "Mas-tur-bate." Miss Rogers smiles and says,

"Wow, Sarah, that's a mouthful." Sarah says, "No, Miss Rogers, you're thinking of a blowjob."

Yo momma is so fat, when she sat on an iPod, she made the iPad!

A young woman was taking golf lessons and had just started playing her first round of golf when she suffered a bee sting. Her pain was so intense that she decided to return to the clubhouse for medical assistance. The golf pro saw her heading back and said, "You are back early, what's wrong?" "I was stung by a bee!" she said. "Where?" he asked. "Between the first and second hole." she replied. He nodded and said, "Your stance is far too wide."

A blonde, wanting to earn some money, decided to hire herself out as a handyman-type and started canvassing a wealthy neighborhood. She went to the front door of the first house and asked the owner if he had any jobs for her to do. "Well, you can paint my porch. How much will you charge?" The blonde said, "How about 50 dollars?" The man agreed and told her that the paint and ladders that she might need were in the garage. The man's wife, inside the house, heard the conversation and said to her husband, "Does she realize that the porch goes all the way around the house?" The man replied, "She should. She was standing on the porch." A short time later, the blonde came to the door to collect her money. "You're finished already?" he asked. "Yes," the blonde answered, "and I had paint left over, so I gave it two coats."Impressed, the man reached in his pocket for the $50. "And by the way," the blonde added, "that's not a Porch, it's a Ferrari."

A woman gets on a bus with her baby. The bus driver says, "That's the ugliest baby that I've ever seen. Ugh!" The woman goes to the rear of the bus and sits down, fuming. She says to a man next to her, "The driver just insulted me!" The man says, "You go right up there and tell him off – go ahead, I'll hold your monkey for you."

After picking her son up from school one day, the mother asks him what he did at school. The kid replies, "I had sex with my teacher." She gets so mad that when they get home, she orders him to go straight to his room. When the father returns home that evening, the mother angrily tells him the news of what their son had done. As the father hears the news, a huge grin spreads across his face. He walks to his son's room and asks him what happened at school, the son tells him, "I had sex with my teacher." The father tells the boy that he is so proud of him, and he is going to reward him with the bike he has been asking for. On the way to the store, the dad asks his son if he would like to ride his new bike home. His son responds, "No thanks Dad, my butt still hurts."

Yo momma is so hairy, when she went to the movie theater to see Star Wars, everybody screamed and said, "IT'S CHEWBACCA!"

Yo mamma is so ugly when she took a bath the water jumped out.

A husband exclaims to his wife one day, "Your butt is getting really big. It's bigger than the BBQ grill!" Later that night in bed, the husband makes some advances towards his wife who completely brushes him off. "What's wrong?" he asks. She answers, "Do you really think I'm going to fire up this big-ass grill for one little weenie?"

One day, there were two boys playing by a stream. One of the young boys saw a bush and went over to it. The other boy couldn't figure out why his friend was at the bush for so long. The other boy went over to the bush and looked. The two boys were looking at a woman bathing naked in the stream. All of a sudden, the second boy took off running. The first boy couldn't understand why he ran away, so he took off after his friend. Finally, he caught up to him and asked why he ran away. The boy said to his friend, "My mom told me if I ever saw a naked lady, I would turn to stone, and I felt something getting hard, so I ran."

Light travels faster than sound. This is why some people appear bright until you hear them speak.

What is the difference between a Mexican and a book? A book has papers.

Yo momma's so dumb, when y'all were driving to Disneyland; she saw a sign that said "Disneyland left," so she went home.

There are 11 people hanging onto a rope that comes down from an airplane. 10 of them are blonde, and one is a brunette. They all decide that one person should get off because if they don't, the rope will break and everyone will die. No one can decide who should go, so finally the brunette delivers a very touching speech, ending with the words, "I'll get off." The blondes, all moved by the brunette's speech, start clapping. Problem solved.

A little boy caught his mom and dad having sex. After, he asked, "What were you and daddy doing?" The mom said, "We were baking a cake." A few days later, the little boy asked his mom, "Were you and daddy baking a cake?" She said yes, and asked him how he knew. He answered, "Because I licked the frosting off the couch."

Yo Momma's so fat when I told her to touch her toes she said, "What are those"?

Q: Why was six scared of seven?
A: Because seven "ate" nine.

A guy was driving in a car with a blonde. He told her to stick her head out the window and see if the blinker worked. She stuck her head out and said, "Yes, No, Yes, No, Yes..."

Q. What did the elephant say to the naked man? A. "How do you breathe through something so small?"

There is a black man, a white man, and a Mexican man on a plane that is too heavy to fly and they are about to crash. They each have to throw something off the plane to save them from crashing. The black man throws out his Jordan shoes and says, "We have too many in our country." The Mexican tosses out his lawn mower and says, "We have too many in our country." The white man puts his item down, grabs the Mexican, throws him out the window and says, "We have too many in our country."

Two cowboys are out on the range talking about their favorite sex position. One says, "I think I enjoy the rodeo position the best." "I don't think I have ever heard of that one," says the other cowboy. "What is it?" "Well, it's where you get your girl down on all four, and you mount her from behind. Then you reach around, cup her tits, and whisper in her ear, 'boy these feel almost as nice as your sisters.' Then you try and hold on for 30 seconds."

A guy walks into a pub and sees a sign hanging over the bar which reads, "Cheese Sandwich: $1.50; Chicken

Sandwich: $2.50; Hand Job: $10.00." Checking his wallet for the necessary payment, he walks up to the bar and beckons to one of the three exceptionally attractive blondes serving drinks to an eager-looking group of men. "Yes?" she enquires with a knowing smile, "Can I help you?" "I was wondering," whispers the man, "Are you the one who gives the hand jobs?" "Yes," she purrs, "I am." The man replies, "Well, go wash your hands, I want a cheese sandwich!"

What did the blonde say when she saw the Cheerios box? "Omg, donut seeds!"

Yo mamma is so fat she doesn't need the internet, because she's already worldwide.

Little Sally came home from school with a smile on her face, and told her mother, "Frankie Brown showed me his weenie today at the playground!" Before the mother could raise a concern, Sally went on to say, "It reminded me of a peanut." Relaxing with a hidden smile, Sally's mom asked, "Really small, was it?" Sally replied, "No, salty." Mom fainted.

There was a preacher who fell in the ocean and he couldn't swim. When a boat came by, the captain yelled, "Do you need help, sir?" The preacher calmly said "No, God will save me." A little later, another boat came by and a fisherman asked, "Hey, do you need help?" The preacher replied again, "No God will save me." Eventually the preacher drowned & went to heaven. The preacher asked God, "Why didn't you save me?" God replied, "Fool, I sent you two boats!"

A blonde goes into a nearby store and asks a clerk if she can buy the TV in the corner. The clerk looks at her and says that he doesn't serve blondes, so she goes back home and dyes her hair black. The next day she returns to the store and asks the same thing, and again, the clerk said he doesn't serve blondes. Frustrated, the blonde goes home and dyes her hair yet again, to a shade of red. Sure that a clerk would sell her the TV this time, she returns and asks a different clerk this time. To her astonishment, this clerk also says that she doesn't serve blondes. The blonde asks the clerk, "How in the world do you know I am a blonde?" The clerk looks at her disgustedly and says, "That's not a TV, it's a microwave!"

A lady goes to the doctor and complains that her husband is losing interest in sex. The doctor gives her a pill, but warns her that it's still experimental. He tells her to slip it into his mashed potatoes at dinner, so that night, she does just that. About a week later, she's back at the doctor, where she says, "Doc, the pill worked great! I put it in the potatoes like you said! It wasn't five minutes later that he jumped up, raked all the food and dishes onto the floor, grabbed me, ripped all my clothes off, and ravaged me right there on the table!" The doctor says, "I'm sorry, we didn't realize the pill was that strong! The foundation will be glad to pay for any damages." "Nah," she says, "that's okay. We're never going back to that restaurant anyway."

Yo momma is so fat that when she saw a yellow school bus go by full of white kids she ran after it yelling, "TWINKIE!"

Q: What's the difference between a Jew and a boy scout?
A: A boy scout comes home from camp.

A blind guy on a bar stool shouts to the bartender, "Wanna hear a blonde joke?" In a hushed voice, the guy next to him says, "Before you tell that joke, you should know something. Our bartender is blonde, the bouncer is blonde. I'm a six foot tall, 200 lb black belt. The guy sitting next to me is six foot two, weighs 225, and he's a rugby player. The fella to your right is six foot five, pushing 300, and he's a wrestler. Each one of us is blonde. Think about it, Mister. Do you still wanna tell that joke?" The blind guy says, "Nah, not if I'm gonna have to explain it five times."

An elderly couple is in church. The wife leans over and whispers to her husband, "I just let out a long, silent fart. What should I do?" The husband replies, "First off, replace the batteries in your hearing aid!"

Q: What do a Christmas tree and a priest have in common?
A: Their balls are just for decoration.

Yo momma is so fat when she went to KFC the cashier asked, "What size bucket?" and yo momma said, "The one on the roof."

There is a cucumber, a pickle, and a penis. They are complaining about their lives. The cucumber says, "My life sucks. I'm put in salads, and to top it off, they put ranch on me as well. My life sucks." The pickle says, "That's nothing compared to my life. I'm put in vinegar and stored away. Boy my life boring. I hate life." The penis says, "Why are you guys complaining? My life is so messed up that I feel like shooting myself. They put me in a plastic bag, put me in a cave, and make me do push-ups until I throw up."

A trucker who has been out on the road for two months stops at a brothel outside Atlanta. He walks straight up to the Madam, drops down $500 and says, "I want your ugliest woman and a grilled cheese sandwich!" The Madam is astonished. "But sir, for that kind of money you could have one of my prettiest ladies and a three-course meal." The trucker replies, "Listen darlin', I'm not horny – I'm just homesick."

"Babe is it in?" "Yea." "Does it hurt?" "Uh huh." "Let me put it in slowly." "It still hurts." "Okay, let's try another shoe size."

Bob was in trouble. He forgot his wedding anniversary. His wife was really pissed. She told him "Tomorrow morning, I expect to find a gift in the driveway that goes from 0 to 200 in 6 seconds AND IT BETTER BE THERE!!" The next morning he got up early and left for work. When his wife woke up, she looked out the window and sure enough there was a box gift-wrapped in the middle of the driveway. Confused, the wife put on her robe and ran out to the driveway, brought the box back in the house. She opened it and found a brand new bathroom scale. Bob has been missing since Friday.

There was an old couple lying in bed. The man turns and tells the woman, "If you want to have sex, pull on my dick once. If you don't want to have sex, pull on my dick one hundred times."

Yo momma so stupid she stuck a battery up her ass and said, "I GOT THE POWER!"

Yo momma is so poor I saw her kicking a trash can so I asked, "What are you doing?" and she said, "I'm moving."

A black guy walks into a bar with a parrot on his shoulder and asks for a beer. The bartender brings a beer and notices the parrot on his shoulder and says, "Hey that's really neat. Where did you get it?" The parrot responds, "In the jungle, there are millions of them."

Q: What is the difference between snowmen and snowwomen?
A: Snowballs.

What is a Mexican's favorite sport? Cross-country.

How did the medical community come up with the term "PMS"? "Mad Cow Disease" was already taken.

Yo momma is so ugly even Hello Kitty said, "Goodbye" to her

Why did the blonde tip toe near the medicine cabinet? Because she didn't want to wake the sleeping pills!!

Your momma's so ugly, when she goes into a strip club; they pay her to keep her clothes on.

A typical macho man married a typical good looking lady, and after the wedding, he laid down the following rules. "I'll be home when I want, if I want, what time I want, and I don't expect any hassle from you. I expect a great dinner to be on the table, unless I tell you that I won't be home for dinner. I'll go hunting, fishing, boozing, and card playing when I want with my old buddies, and don't you give me a hard time about it. Those are my rules. Any comments?" His new bride said, "No, that's fine with me. Just understand that there will be sex here at seven o'clock every night, whether you're here or not."

My friend thinks he is smart. He told me an onion is the only food that makes you cry, so I threw a coconut at his face.

Yo momma is so stupid when your dad sad it was chilly outside, she ran out the door with a spoon!

Q: How many Mexicans does it take to change a light bulb?
A: Just Juan.

Yo momma is so fat she sat on the rainbow and Skittles came out.

A woman places an ad in the local newspaper. "Looking for a man with three qualifications: won't beat me up, won't run away from me, and is great in bed." Two days later her doorbell rings. "Hi, I'm Tim. I have no arms so I won't beat you, and no legs so I won't run away." "What makes you think you are great in bed?" the woman retorts. Tim replies, "I rang the doorbell, didn't I?"

It was Christmas Eve. A woman came home to her husband after a day of busy shopping. Later on that night when she was getting undressed for bed, he noticed a mark on the inside of her leg. "What is that?" he asked. She said, "I visited the tattoo parlor today. On the inside of one leg I had them tattoo 'Merry Christmas,' and on the inside of the other one they tattooed 'Happy New Year.'" Perplexed, he asked, "Why did you do that?" "Well," she replied, "now you can't complain that there's never anything to eat between Christmas and New Years!"

Q: What do you call a bear with no teeth?
A: A gummy bear.

There was a papa mole, a momma mole, and a baby mole. They lived in a hole out in the country near a farmhouse. Papa mole poked his head out of the hole and said, "Mmmm, I smell sausage!" Momma mole poked her head outside the hole and said, "Mmmm, I smell pancakes!" Baby mole tried to stick his head outside but couldn't because of the two bigger moles. Baby mole said, "The only thing I smell is molasses."

After Brian proposed to Jill, his father took him to one side. "Son, when I first got married to your mother, the first thing I did when we got home was take off my pants. I gave them to your mother and told her to try them on, which she did. They were huge on her and she said that she couldn't wear them because they were too large. I said to her, 'Of course they are too big for you, I wear the pants in this family and I always will.' Ever since that day, son, we have never had a single problem." Brian took his dad's advice and did the same thing to his wife on his wedding night. Then, Jill took off her panties and gave them to Brian. "Try these on," she said. Brian went along with it and tried them on, but they were far too small. "What's the point of this? I can't get into your panties," said Brian. "Exactly," Jill replied, "and if you don't change your attitude, you never will!"

Q: Why do black people hate country music?
A: Because when they hear the word "hoedown" they think their sister got shot.

I never wanted to believe that my Dad was stealing from his job as a road worker. But when I got home, all the signs were there.

Why did Hitler kill himself? Because he saw his gas bill.

A little kids sends a letter to Santa that says: "Dear Santa I want a brother for Christmas." Santa writes back, "Dear Timmy send me me your mommy."

A cowboy walks into a bar, sits down, and asks for a shot. Across the bar, a Mexican man is sitting and glaring at the cowboy. The cowboy takes the shot and slams the shot glass down on the counter, yelling, "TGIF!" The Mexican orders a shot, takes it, and slams his glass down, yelling, "SPIT!" The cowboy looks over at him and notices the Mexican guy is still staring at him. The cowboy once again orders a shot, slams it down, and yells again "TGIF!" Once again, the Mexican orders a shot, slams it down after consuming it, and yells out, "SPIT!" This goes on for a while, and the bartender stands puzzled and annoyed. Finally, the bartender asks the cowboy, "Just checking, but do you know what TGIF means?" and the cowboy replies, "Hell ya I know what it means, 'Thank God It's Friday!'" The bartender asks the Mexican guy, "Okay, so what does 'SPIT' mean?" and the Mexican replies, "Stupid Pendejo It's Thursday!"

A man is talking to God. "God, how long is a million years?" God answers, "To me, it's about a minute." "God, how much is a million dollars?" "To me, it's a penny." "God, may I have a penny?" "Wait a minute."

A police officer stops a blonde for speeding and asks if he could see her license. She replied in a huff, "I wish you guys could get your act together. Just yesterday you take away my license and then today you expect me to show it to you."

A blonde goes to the doctor's and find out she is pregnant with twins. She starts crying and the doctor asks her what's wrong. She replies, "I know who the dad is for one of them but I don't know who the dad is for the other one!"

Two bats are hanging upside down on a branch. One asks the other, "Do you recall your worst day last year?" The other responds, "Yes, the day I had diarrhea!"

Three guys go to a ski lodge, and there aren't enough rooms, so they have to share a bed. In the middle of the night, the guy on the right wakes up and says, "I had this wild, vivid dream of getting a hand job!" The guy on the left wakes up, and unbelievably, he's had the same dream, too. Then the guy in the middle wakes up and says, "That's funny, I dreamed I was skiing!"

Why did the blonde put her iPad in a blender? Because she wanted to make apple juice.

Yo momma is so stupid she took a ruler to bed to see how long she slept.

A few days after Christmas, a mother was working in the kitchen listening to her young son playing with his new electric train in the living room. She heard the train stop and her son said, "All of you sons of bitches who want off, get the hell off now, because this is the last stop! And all of you sons of bitches, who are getting on, get your asses in the train, because we're going down the tracks." The mother went nuts and told her son, "We don't use that kind of language in this house. Now I want you to go to your room and you are to stay there for TWO HOURS. When you come out, you may play with your train, but I want you to use nice language." Two hours later, the son comes out of the bedroom and resumes playing with his train. Soon the train stopped and the mother heard her son say, "All passengers who are disembarking from the train please remember to take all of your belongings with you. We thank you for riding with us today and hope your trip was a pleasant one. We hope you will ride with us again soon." She hears the little boy continue, "For those of you just boarding, we ask you to stow all of your hand luggage under your seat. Remember, there is no smoking on the train. We hope you will have a pleasant and relaxing journey with us today." As the mother began to smile, the child added, "For those of you who are pissed off about the two hour delay, please see the bitch in the kitchen."

Ralph is driving home one evening, when he suddenly realizes that it's his daughter's birthday and he hasn't bought her a present. He drives to the mall, runs to the toy store, and says to the shop assistant, "How much is that Barbie in the window?" In a condescending manner, she says, "Which Barbie?" She continues, "We have Barbie Goes to the Gym for $19.95, Barbie Goes to the Ball for $19.95, Barbie Goes Shopping for $19.95, Barbie Goes to the Beach for $19.95, Barbie Goes Nightclubbing for $19.95, and Divorced Barbie for $265.00." Ralph asks, "Why is the Divorced Barbie $265.00 when all the others are only $19.95?" "That's obvious," the saleslady says. "Divorced Barbie comes with Ken's house, Ken's car, Ken's boat, Ken's furniture..."

How do you get the little black kids to stop jumping on the bed? Put Velcro on the ceiling. How do you get them down? Tell the Mexican kids it's a piñata.

A man asks, "God, why did you make woman so beautiful?" God responded,"So you would love her." The man asks, "But God, why did you make her so dumb?" God replied, "So she would love you."

Yo momma is so fat when she stepped on the scale it read, "Get the hell off me!"

A blonde, out of money, and down on her luck after buying air at a real bargain, needed money desperately. To raise cash, she decided to kidnap a child and hold him for ransom. She went to the local playground, grabbed a kid randomly, took her behind a building, and told her, "I've kidnapped you." She then wrote a big note saying, "I've kidnapped your kid. Tomorrow morning, put $10,000 in a paper bag and leave it under the apple tree next to the slides, on the south side of the playground. Signed, a blonde." The blonde then pinned the note to the kid's shirt and sent him home to show it to his parents. The next morning, the blonde checked, and sure enough, a paper bag was sitting beneath the apple tree. The blonde looked in the bag and found the $10,000 with a note that said, "How could you do this to a fellow blonde?"

A US Border Patrol Agent catches an illegal alien in the bushes right by the border fence, he pulls him out and says "Sorry, you know the law, you've got to go back across the border right now." The Mexican man pleads with them, "No, noooo Senor, I must stay in de USA! Pleeeze!" The Border Patrol Agent thinks to himself, I'm going to make it hard for him and says "Ok, I'll let you stay if you can use three English words in a sentence. The three words are 'green,' 'pink,' and 'yellow.'" The Mexican man thinks, then says, "Hmmm, okay. The phone, it went green, green, green. I pink it up and sez yellow?"

Did you hear about the two bald guys who put their heads together? They made an ass out of themselves!

Three brothers are traveling along a road, and their car dies. They all get out of the car, and start walking to a barn that's a little ways away. When they get there, the farmer comes out of the barn, and offers them a room for one night. He says to the first one, "You can sleep with the pigs," the second guy," you can sleep with the cows", and the third guy, "I like the cut of your jib. You can sleep with my 18 daughters." The next morning, he asks everyone how they slept. The first man said, "I slept like a pig." The second man said,"I slept like a cow." The third guy said, "I slept like a rabbit. I jumped from hole, to hole, to hole."

Yo momma so fat when she steps out in a yellow raincoat, the people yell, "TAXI!"

Q: What's the difference between a black man and a park bench?
A: A park bench can support a family of four.

Q: Which sexual position produces the ugliest children?
A: Ask your mother.

A man goes to a bar and sees a fat girl dancing on a table. He walks over to her and says, "Wow, nice legs!" She is flattered and replies, "You really think so?" The man says, "Oh definitely! Most tables would have collapsed by now."

A lawyer married a woman who had previously divorced 10 husbands. On their wedding night, she told her new husband, "Please be gentle, I'm still a virgin." "What?" said the puzzled groom. "How can that be if you've been married 10 times?" "Well, Husband #1 was a sales representative. He kept telling me how great it was going to be. Husband #2 was in software services. He was never really sure how it was supposed to function, but he said he'd look into it and get back to me. Husband #3 was from field services. He said everything checked out diagnostically, but he just couldn't get the system up. Husband #4 was in telemarketing. Even though he knew he had the order, he didn't know when he would be able to deliver. Husband #5 was an engineer. He understood the basic process, but wanted three years to research, implement, and design a new state-of-the-art method. Husband #6 was from finance and administration. He thought he knew how, but he wasn't sure whether it was his job or not. Husband #7 was in marketing. Although he had a nice product, he was never sure how to position it. Husband #8 was a psychologist. All he ever did was talk about it. Husband #9 was a gynecologist. All he did was look at it. Husband #10 was a stamp collector. All he ever did was... God! I miss him! But now that I've married you, I'm really excited!" "Good," said the new husband, "but, why?" "You're a lawyer. This time I know I'm going to get screwed!"

What do you call a black man flying a plane? A pilot, you racist.

A woman goes to her boyfriend's parents' house for dinner. This is her first time meeting the family and she is very nervous. They all sit down and begin eating a fine meal. The woman is beginning to feel a little discomfort, thanks to her nervousness and the broccoli casserole. The gas pains are almost making her eyes water. Left with no other choice, she decides to relieve herself a bit and lets out a dainty little fart. It wasn't loud, but everyone at the table heard the poot. Before she even had a chance to be embarrassed, her boyfriend's father looked over at the dog that had been snoozing at the women's feet, and said in a rather stern voice, "Ginger!" The woman thought, "This is great!" and a big smile came across her face. A couple minutes later, she was beginning to feel the pain again. This time, she didn't hesitate. She let a much louder and longer fart rip. The father again looked at the dog and yelled, "Dammit, Ginger!" Once again the woman smiled and thought, "Yes!" A few minutes later the woman had to let another one rip. This time she didn't even think about it. She let rip a fart that rivaled a train whistle blowing. Again, the father looked at the dog with disgust and yelled, "Dammit, Ginger, get away from her before she shits on you!"

A brunette and blonde are walking in the park when the brunette says, "Aw, look at the dead birdie." The blonde looks up and says, "Where?"

Yo momma's so fat, that when she went to the zoo, the hippos got jealous.

There were three guys in Hell - Iranian, American, and a Chinese man. They asked Satan to let them call their family. The American called and talked for 10 minutes. He payed $1,000. The Chinaman called and talked for 15 minutes. He payed $2,000. The Iranian talked for an hour and only paid $10. The other men complained and Satan responded, "A call from Hell to Hell is local."

Q: How do you count cows?
A: With a cowculator.

A woman is having a hard time getting her tomatoes to ripen so she goes to her neighbor with her problem. The neighbor says, "All you have to do is go out at midnight and dance around in the garden naked for a few minutes, and the tomatoes will become so embarrassed, they will blush bright red." The woman goes out at midnight and dances around her garden naked for a few minutes. The next morning, the neighbor comes over to the woman's house and asks the woman if her tomatoes have turned red. The woman says "No, they're still green, but I noticed the cucumbers grew four inches!"

I asked a Chinese girl for her number. She said, "Sex! Sex! Sex! Free sex tonight!" I said, "Wow!" Then her friend said, "She means 666-3629."

Yo momma so ugly, she had to get the baby drunk so that she could breastfeed it.

Why did so many black men get killed in Vietnam? When the generals would yell, "Get down!" they would all start dancing.

Q: Why couldn't the blonde add 10 + 5 on a calculator?
A: She couldn't find the "10" button.

What do you call a Jewish homosexual? A He-blew.

Yo mama's so stupid she put paper on the television and called it paper view.

A tough looking group of hairy bikers are riding when they see a girl about to jump off a bridge, so they stop. The leader, a big burly man, gets off his bike and says, "What are you doing?" "I'm going to commit suicide," she says. While he doesn't want to appear insensitive, he also doesn't want to miss an opportunity, so he asks, "Well, before you jump, why don't you give me a kiss?" She does, and it is a long, deep, lingering kiss. After she's finished, the tough, hairy biker says, "Wow! That was the best kiss I've ever had! That's a real talent you're wasting. You could be famous. Why are you committing suicide?" "My parents don't like me dressing up like a girl…"

An old couple is ready to go to sleep. The old man lies on the bed but the old woman lies down on the floor. The old man asks, "Why are you going to sleep on the floor?" The old woman says, "Because I want to feel something hard for a change."

Three blondes walk into a building. You'd think one of them would've seen it.....

A man buys a lie detector robot that slaps people who lie. He decides to test it at dinner. He asks his son, "Son, where were you today during school hours?" "At school." The robot slaps the son. "Okay, I went to the movies!" The father asks, "Which one?" "Harry Potter." The robot slaps the son again. "Okay, I was watching porn!" The father replies, "What? When I was your age I didn't even know what porn was!" The robot slaps the father. The mom chimes in, "Ha-ha! After all, he is your son!" The robot slaps the mother.

I was sitting on my own in a restaurant, when I saw a beautiful woman at another table. I sent her a bottle of the most expensive wine on the menu. She sent me a note, "I will not touch a drop of this wine unless you can assure me that you have seven inches in your pocket." I wrote back, "Give me the wine. As gorgeous as you are, I'm not cutting off three inches for anyone."

Did you hear about the blonde that got excited? She finished a jigsaw puzzle in six months, when the box said, "two to four years."

Yo momma is so ashy, every time she rubs her arms it snows.

Yo momma's so fat, she has more rolls than a bakery.

There was a redneck who hit every black man he saw with his truck. One day he saw a priest walking down the road and thought, "For all the bad things I done, let me give this priest a ride." So he picked the priest up and they drove along. The redneck saw a black guy down the road and decided he would pretend to fall asleep and so the priest would think it was an accident. The redneck closed his eyes and heard a loud bang. "What happened?" he asked. "You missed him," the priest said, "but I got him with the door."

Yo momma is so ugly she turned Medusa into stone.

Wife: "In my dream, I saw you in a jewelry store and you bought me a diamond ring."
Husband: "I had the same dream and I saw your dad paying the bill."

A gynecologist notices that a new patient is nervous. While putting on the latex gloves, he asks her if she knows how they make latex gloves. The patient says no. The doctor says, "There is a plant in Mexico full of latex that people of various hand sizes dip their hands into and let them dry. She does not crack a smile, but later she laughs. The doctor says, "What's so funny?" She says, "I'm imagining how they make condoms."

For all the guys who think a woman's place is in the kitchen, remember that's where the knives are kept.

My uncle was a racist piano player, all his work sounded awful because he skipped all the black keys.

How can you tell when a brunette is actually a blonde who dyes her hair? When she trips over the cordless phone.

A blonde is watching the news with her husband when the newscaster says, "Six Brazilian men die in a skydiving accident." The blonde starts crying to her husband, sobbing, "That's horrible!" Confused, he replies, "Yes Dear, it is sad, but they were skydiving, and there is always that risk involved." After a few minutes, the blonde, still sobbing, says, "How many is a Brazilian?"

An organization is like a tree full of monkeys, all on different limbs at different levels. The monkeys on top look down and see a tree full of smiling faces. The monkeys on the bottom look up and see nothing but assholes.

School is like a boner. It's long and hard unless you're Asian.

Q: What did the blanket say when it fell of the bed?
A: "Oh sheet!"

Yo momma's so fat, the only way to get her out of a telephone booth is to grease her thighs and throw a Twinkie in the street.

There is a fellow who is talking to his buddy and says, "I don't know what to get my wife for her birthday. She has everything, and besides, she can afford to buy anything she wants. I'm stumped." His buddy says, "I have an idea. Why don't you make up a certificate that says she can have two hours of great sex, any way she wants it. She'll probably be thrilled!" The first fellow does just that. The next day, his buddy asks, "Well, did you take my suggestion? How did it turn out?" "She loved it. She jumped up, thanked me, kissed me on the mouth, and ran out the door yelling, 'I'll see you in two hours!'"

Did you hear they finally made a device that makes cars run 95% quieter? Yeah, it fits right over her mouth.

"May I take your order?" the blonde waitress asked. "Yes, how do you prepare your chickens?" "Nothing special sir," she replied, "we just tell them straight out that they're going to die."

78% of black men like sex in the shower. The other 22% haven't been to prison yet.

You are on a horse, galloping at a constant speed. On your right side is a sharp drop off, and on your left side is an elephant traveling at the same speed as you. Directly in front of you is another galloping horse but your horse is unable to overtake it. Behind you is a lion running at the same speed as you and the horse in front of you. What must you do to safely get out of this highly dangerous situation? Get your drunk ass off the merry-go-round!

How do you starve a black person? Put their food stamp card under their work boots!

Yo momma's so fat she can't even jump to a conclusion.

How did the Mexican girl get pregnant? Her teacher told her to do an essay.

Yo momma's so fat, she got baptized at Sea World.

A man escapes from prison where he has been for 15 years. He breaks into a house to look for money and guns, and finds a young couple in bed. He orders the guy out of bed and ties him to a chair. He ties the girl to the bed and he gets on top of her, kisses her neck, and then gets up and goes into the bathroom. While he's in there, the husband tells his wife, "Listen, this guy is an escaped convict, look at his clothes! He probably spent lots of time in jail and hasn't seen a woman in years. I saw how he kissed your neck. If he wants sex, don't resist, don't complain, do whatever he tells you. Satisfy him no matter how much he nauseates you. This guy is probably very dangerous. If he gets angry, he'll kill us. Be strong, honey. I love you." His wife responds, "He wasn't kissing my neck. He was whispering in my ear. He told me he was gay, thought you were cute, and asked me if we had any Vaseline. I told him it was in the bathroom. Be strong honey. I love you, too!"

Yo momma is so short; you can see her feet on her driver's license.

In a Catholic school cafeteria, a nun places a note in front of a pile of apples, "Only take one. God is watching." Further down the line is a pile of cookies. A little boy makes his own note, "Take all you want. God is watching the apples."

"Daddy, where did I come from?" seven-year-old Rachel asks. It is a moment for which her parents have carefully prepared. They take her into the living room, get out several other books, and explain all they think she should know about sexual attraction, affection, love, and reproduction. Then they both sit back and smile contentedly. "Does that answer your question?" the mom asks. "Not really," the little girl says. "Judy said she came from Detroit. I want to know where I came from."

Jesus, Moses, and an old man go golfing. The first one to tee off is Moses. He smashes the ball and it is heading right for the water hazard before the green. Moses raises his club, the water parts, and the ball makes it to the green. Jesus gets up to swing, cranks it out, and it is headed for the water hazard. Jesus closes his eyes and prays. The ball skips across the water and lands on the green two feet from the hole. The old man's turn comes and he drives the ball. The ball looks like it is going to drop directly into the water. A fish jumps from the water hazard swallowing the ball, as an eagle drops from the sky, grabbing the fish. As the eagle flies over the green, a bolt of lightning strikes the eagle, making it drop the fish. As the fish hits the green, it spits out the ball and the ball falls into the hole, making a hole in one. Jesus looks at Moses and says, "I really think I'm leaving Dad at home next time!"

There are three blondes who are on a road trip. As they are driving through the desert, their car breaks down. They have no phone to call anyone, so they decide to walk to the nearest city, several miles away. They each decide to take one thing to make the journey better. The first blonde takes the radio and says, "If we get bored, we can put the radio on and listen to music." The second blonde decides to take a wheel, "In case one of us gets really tired, we can go inside the wheel and be rolled." The third blonde takes the car door, "In case it gets too hot, we can roll down the window!"

Q: Why can't Mexicans play Uno?
A: They always steal the green cards.

So I asked a blonde, "Which is closer, Florida or the Sun?" She said, "The Sun, because I can look up and see it.

A drunk staggers into a Catholic Church, enters a confessional booth, sits down, but says nothing. The Priest coughs a few times to get his attention, but the drunk continues to sit there. Finally, the Priest pounds three times on the wall. The drunk mumbles, "Ain't no use knockin'! There's no paper on this side either!"

How did the blonde die drinking milk? The cow fell on her.

A guy and his date are parked out in the country away from town, when they start kissing and fondling each other. Just then, the girl stops and sits up. "What's the matter?" asks the guy. She replies, "I really should have mentioned this earlier, but I'm actually a prostitute, and I charge $100 for sex." The man thinks about it for a few seconds, but then reluctantly gets out a $100 bill, pays her, and they have sex. After a cigarette, he just sits in the driver's seat looking out the window. "Why aren't we going anywhere?" asks the girl. "Well, I should have mentioned this before," replies the man, "but I'm actually a taxi driver, and the fare back to town is $50.

A lawyer runs a stop sign and gets pulled over by a sheriff. He thinks he's smarter being a big shot lawyer from New York and has a better education than a sheriff from West Virginia. The sheriff asks for license and registration. The lawyer asks, "What for?" The sheriff responds, "You didn't come to a complete stop at the stop sign." The lawyer says, "I slowed down and no one was coming." "You still didn't come to a complete stop. License and registration please," say the sheriff impatiently. The lawyer says, "If you can show me the legal difference between slow down and stop, I'll give you my license and registration and you can give me the ticket. If not, you let me go and don't give me the ticket." The sheriff says, "That sounds fair, please exit your vehicle." The lawyer steps out and the sheriff takes out his nightstick and starts beating the lawyer with it. The sheriff says, "Do you want me to stop or just slow down?"

Yo momma is so ugly Fix-It Felix said, "I can't fix it."

There is an overweight guy who is watching TV. A commercial comes on for a guaranteed weight loss of 10 pounds in a week. So the guy, thinking what the hell, signs up for it. Next morning an incredibly beautiful woman is standing at his door in nothing but a pair of running shoes and a sign about her neck that reads, "If you can catch me, you can have me." As soon as he sees her, she takes off running. He tries to catch her, but is unable. This continues for a week, at the end of which, the man has lost 10 pounds. After this he tries the next weight loss plan, 15 pounds in a week. The next morning an even more beautiful woman is standing at the door, in similar conditions. The same happens with her as the first woman, except he almost catches her. This continues for a week, at the end of which he, as suspected, weighs 15 pounds less. Excited about this success, he decides to do the master program. Before he signs up, he is required to sign a waiver and is warned about the intensity of this plan. Still he signs up. The next morning, waiting at the door, is a hulking 300 pound muscle man with nothing but a pair of running shoes, a raging erection, and a sign around his neck that says, "If I catch you, you're mine!" The man was supposed to lose 25 pounds in the week; he lost 34.

During a discussion at Sunday school, a nun asks the children what they think God takes you by when you die. A kid responds, "I think God takes you by your feet, because once I walked into my parents room and my mom's feet were in the air and she was screaming, "Oh God, I'm coming!!!"

I was at my bank today waiting in a short line. There was just one lady in front of me, an Asian lady, who was trying to exchange yen for dollars. It was obvious she was a little irritated. She asked the teller, "Why it change? Yesterday, I get two hunat dolla of yen. Today I only get hunat eighty? Why it change?" The teller shrugged his shoulders and said, "Fluctuations." The Asian lady says, "Fluc you white people too!"

A blonde really got tired of all blonde jokes and decided to hang herself in the bathroom. As she locked the door, she yelled at her husband, "I'm hanging myself because I'm tired of jokes about us blondes being stupid!" Her husband broke into the bathroom and saw his wife with a rope tied on her toe. The husband said, "I thought you were hanging yourself." She said, "Yes, I am!" The husband replied, "Usually when people hang themselves, they tie the rope around their neck, so why is yours tied on your toe?" She said, "I tried that, but I couldn't breathe."

Josey wasn't the best pupil at Sunday school. She often fell asleep and one day while she was sleeping, the teacher asked her a question. "Who is the creator of the universe?" Joe was sitting next to Josey and decided to poke her with a pin to wake her up. Josey jumped and yelled, "God almighty!" The teacher congratulated her. A little later the teacher asked her another question, "Tell me who is our lord and savior?" Joe poked Josey again and she yelled out, "Jesus Christ!" The teacher congratulated her again. Later on the teacher asked, "What did Eve say to Adam after their 26th child?" Joe poked Josey again and she shouted, "If you stick that thing in me again, I'll snap it in half and stick it up your ass!"

Q: Why did President Obama get two terms?
A: Because every black man gets a longer sentence.

Yo mamma is so fat she walked past the TV and I missed 3 episodes.

A teacher asked her students to use the word "beans" in a sentence. "My father grows beans," said one girl. "My mother cooks beans," said a boy. A third student spoke up, "We are all human beans."

A proud and confident genius makes a bet with an idiot. The genius says, "Hey idiot, every question I ask you that you don't know the answer, you have to give me $5. And if you ask me a question and I can't answer yours I will give you $5,000." The idiot says, "Okay." The genius then asks, "How many continents are there in the world?" The idiot doesn't know and hands over the $5. The idiot says, "Now me ask: what animal stands with two legs but sleeps with three?" The genius tries and searches very hard for the answer but gives up and hands over the $5000. The genius says, "Dang it, I lost. By the way, what was the answer to your question?" The idiot hands over $5.

Q: When is the only time you can smack an ugly woman in the face?
A: When her mustache is on fire.

What did the blonde say when she found out she was pregnant? I wonder if it's mine.

Q: Why is sex like math?
A: You add a bed, subtract the clothes, divide the legs, and pray there's no multiplying.

Two bored casino dealers are waiting at the craps table. A very attractive blonde woman from South Alabama arrives and bets $20,000 on a single roll of dice. She says, "I hope you don't mind, but I feel much luckier when I play topless." With that, she strips to the waist, rolls the dice, and yells, "Come on, Southern girl needs new clothes!" As the dice bounce and come to a stop, she jumps up and down and squeals, "Yes! Yes! I won! I won!" She hugs each of the dealers, picks up her winnings, and her clothes, and quickly departs. The dealers stare at each other dumbfounded. Finally, one of them asks, "What did she roll?" The other answers, "I don't know, I thought you were watching."

A policeman sees a little girl riding her bike and says, "Did Santa get you that?" "Yes," replies the little girl. "Well," says the policeman, "tell Santa to put a reflector light on it next year," and fines her five dollars. The little girl looks up at the policeman and says, "Nice horse you've got there, did Santa bring you that?" The policeman chuckles and replies, "He sure did!" "Well," says the little girl, "next year, tell Santa the d*ck goes under the horse and not on it."

Yo momma's so smelly, that when she spread her legs, I got seasick.

Yo mama so ugly when she went into a haunted house she came out with a job application.

At school, Little Johnny's classmate tells him that most adults are hiding at least one dark secret, so it's very easy to blackmail them by saying, "I know the whole truth." Little Johnny decides to go home and try it out.

Johnny's mother greets him at home, and he tells her, "I know the whole truth." His mother quickly hands him $20 and says, "Just don't tell your father." Quite pleased, the boy waits for his father to get home from work, and greets him with, "I know the whole truth." The father promptly hands him $40 and says, "Please don't say a word to your mother."

Very pleased, the boy is on his way to school the next day when he sees the mailman at his front door. The boy greets him by saying, "I know the whole truth." The mailman immediately drops the mail, opens his arms, and says, "Then come give your Daddy a great big hug!"

Mr. and Mrs. Brown had two sons. One was named Mind Your Own Business & the other was named Trouble. One day the two boys decided to play hide and seek. Trouble hid while Mind Your Own Business counted to one hundred. Mind Your Own Business began looking for his brother behind garbage cans and bushes. Then he started looking in and under cars until a police man approached him and asked, "What are you doing?" "Playing a game," the boy replied. "What is your name?" the officer questioned. "Mind Your Own Business." Furious the policeman inquired, "Are you looking for trouble?!" The boy replied, "Why, yes."

A wife asked her husband, "What do you like most in me, my pretty face or my sexy body?" He looked at her from head to toe and replied, "I like your sense of humor!"

How was copper wire invented? Two Jews fighting over a penny.

A little boy with diarrhea tells his mom that he needs Viagra. The mom asks, "Why on Earth do you need that?!" The little boy says, "Isn't that what you give daddy when his shit doesn't get hard?"

A guy goes to the store to buy condoms. "Do you want a bag?" the cashier asks. "No," the guy says, "she's not that ugly."

Women might be able to fake orgasms, but men can fake a whole relationship.

Yo momma's so fat, she wore a black bathing suit to the pool and everyone yelled "oil spill!"

How do you confuse a blonde? Put her in a circle and tell her to go to the corner.

Q: What is the difference between an illegal immigrant and E.T.?
A: E.T. eventually went home.

A science teacher tells his class, "Oxygen is a must for breathing and life. It was discovered in 1773." A blonde student responds, "Thank God I was born after 1773! Otherwise I would have died without it."

Yo momma is so fat she uses a pillow for a tampon.

A German asks a Mexican if they have any Jews in Mexico. The Mexican says, "Sí, we have orange jews, apple jews, and grape jews!"

Where do you send Jewish kids with Attention Deficit Disorder? Concentration Camp!

A man is drinking in a bar when he notices a beautiful young lady. "Hello there and what is your name?" "Hello," giggles the woman, "I'm Stacey. What's yours?" "I'm Jim." "Jim, do you want to come over to my house tonight?" "Sure!" replies Jim. "Let's go!" At Stacey's house after having the best sex of his life, Jim notices a picture of a man on Stacey's desk and asks, "Is this your brother?" "No, it isn't, Jim!" Stacey giggles. "Is it your husband?" Stacey giggles even more, "No, silly!" "Then, it must be your boyfriend!" Stacey giggles even more while nibbling on Jim's ear. She says, "No, silly!" "Then, who is it?" Stacey replies, "That's me before my operation!"

What did the left pussy lip say to the right pussy lip? "We used to be really tight until you let that dick come between us."

So a man dies, goes to Heaven, and sees St. Peter. There are many clocks surrounding him so the man asks, "What are these clocks for?" St. Peter replies, "These are lie clocks, they tick once for every lie you tell. Here we have Mother Teresa's clock. She has never lied so the clock has not moved. Honest Abe has only lied twice in his life, so it has only ticked twice." The man then asks, "So where is Barrack Obama's clock?" St. Peter replies, "Oh, that is in Jesus' office, he is using it as a ceiling fan!"

A lady comes home from her doctor's appointment grinning from ear to ear. Her husband asks, "Why are you so happy?" The wife says, "The doctor told me that for a forty-five year old woman, I have the breasts of an eighteen year old." "Oh yeah?" quipped her husband, "What did he say about your forty-five year old ass?" She said, "Your name never came up in the conversation."

A boy asks his dad, "What's the difference between potential and realistic?" The dad tells him to go ask the rest of his family if they'd sleep with Brad Pitt for a million dollars, and then he'd tell him the answer. The boy goes up to his mom and asks her. She responds, "A million dollars is a lot of money sweetheart. I could send you, your sister, and your brother to great colleges, so sure, I would!" He then goes and asks his sister to which she replies, "Brad Pitt? Hell ya, he's the hottest guy ever!" Next, the boy asks his brother who replies, "A million dollars? Hell yes I would. I'd be rich!" When the boy excitedly returns to his dad with the family's responses, the dad says, "Well son, potentially, we have three million dollars. Realistically, we have two sluts and a queer."

Why do Mexican kids eat tamales on Christmas? So they can have something to unwrap.

Instead of "the John," I call my toilet "the Jim." That way it sounds better when I say I go to the Jim first thing every morning.

Tired of constant blonde jokes, a blonde dyes her hair brown. She then goes for a drive in the country and sees a shepherd herding his sheep across the road.
"Hey, shepherd, if I guess how many sheep are here, can I keep one?"
The shepherd is puzzled but agrees. She blurts out "352!" He is stunned but keeps his word and allows her to pick a sheep.

"I'll take this one," she says proudly. "It's the cutest!"
"Hey lady," says the shepherd, "If I guess your real hair color, can I have my dog back?"

If con is the opposite of pro, then is Congress the opposite of progress?

Yo mamma is so ugly, she scared the shit out of the toilet.

What do you call a Mexican with a rubber toe? Roberto

Its game 7 of the NBA finals and a man makes his way to his seat at center court. He sits down and notices that the seat next to him is empty. He leans over and asks his neighbor if someone is sitting there. He responds, "No, the seat's empty." "The first man exclaims, "What?!? Who in their right mind would have a seat like this for the NBA finals and not use it?" The neighbor responds, "Well the seat is mine, but my wife passed away and this is the first NBA finals we haven't been together." The first man responds," I'm sorry to hear that. Wasn't there anyone else, a friend or relative, that could've taken that seat?" The neighbor responds, "No, they're all at the funeral."

Q: How do astronomers organize a party?
A: They planet.

Mexico doesn't win Olympic medals because all the best runners, jumpers, and swimmers are in America.

Why did the blonde like lightening? She thought someone was taking a picture of her.

The bell rang for school to start and John walked in late. Mr. Clark asked, "John, why are you late?" He replied, "I was on Cherry Hill." Then he sat down. Ten minutes later Nathan walked in late and Mr. Clark repeated, "Why are you late?" Nathan answered, "I was on top of Cherry Hill." Five minutes later Kevin walked in late and Mr. Clark said to him, "Kevin, where have you been?" Kevin replied, "I was on Cherry Hill." Ten minutes later a girl walked in the classroom and Mr. Clark asked, "Hi there, what's your name?" The girl replied, "Cherry Hill."

Your momma is so hairy when she opens her legs it says "Welcome to Busch Gardens."

Two factory workers are talking. The woman says, "I can make the boss give me the day off." The man replies, "And how would you do that?" The woman says, "Just wait and see." She then hangs upside down from the ceiling. The boss comes in and says, "What are you doing?" The woman replies, "I'm a light bulb." The boss then says, "You've been working so much that you've gone crazy. I think you need to take the day off." The man starts to follow her and the boss says, "Where are you going?" The man says, "I'm going home, too. I can't work in the dark."

A blonde, a brunette, and a redhead are running from the police. They run into an old barn and hide in potato sacks. The officer chasing them walks into the barn looking for them. He kicks the first sack with the redhead inside and the redhead says, "Woof woof!" The cop thinks it's a dog, so he walks to the next one. He kicks the second bag with the brunette, and she says, "Meow meow!" The cop believes it's a cat and moves on. He kicks the third bag with the blonde, and the blonde yells, "Potato potato!"

How do you know Barbie is not a slut? Because her legs don't open.

Yo momma is so poor that when I asked her what's for dinner tonight she lit her pocket on fire and said, "hot pocket."

An investigative journalist went to Afghanistan to study the culture and was shocked to discover that women were made to walk ten paces behind the men. She asked her guide why and he said, "Because they are considered of lesser status." Outraged the journalist went home. A year later she returned covering violence in the region and was surprised to see the women walking ten paces ahead. She turned to her guide and this time asked, "What has changed?" The guide answered, "Land mines."

An Asian lady went into labor and her child came out black. The doctor asked her if she picked a name for the baby and she said, "Yea, Som Ting Wong!" (Something's wrong)

A blonde is overweight so her doctor puts her on a diet. "I want you to eat regularly for two days, then skip a day and repeat for two weeks and you'll lose at least five pounds." When the blonde returns, she's lost nearly 20 pounds. The doctor exclaims, "That's amazing! Did you follow my diet?" The blonde nods. "I thought I was going to drop dead every third day from all the skipping!"

Yo momma is so fat, when she sat on the back of the bus it did a wheelie.

A man is walking down the street, when he notices that his grandfather is sitting on the porch in a rocking chair, with nothing on from the waist down. "Grandpa, what are you doing?" the man exclaims. The old man looks off in the distance and does not answer his grandson. "Grandpa, what are you doing sitting out here with nothing on below the waist?" he asks again. The old man slyly looks at him and says, "Well, last week I sat out here with no shirt on, and I got a stiff neck. This was your Grandma's idea!"

There's a new drug for lesbians on the market to cure depression, it's called Trycoxagain.

There was this guy at a bar, just looking at his drink. He stays like that for a half hour. Then a big trouble making truck driver steps next to him, takes the drink from the guy, & just drinks it all down. The poor man starts crying. The truck driver says, "Come on man, I was just joking. Here, I'll buy you another drink. I just can't stand to see a man cry." "No, it's not that," the man replies, wiping his tears, "This day is the worst of my life. First, I oversleep & I go in late to my office. My outraged boss fires me. When I leave the building to go to my car, I find out it was stolen. The police say they can do nothing. I get a cab to go home, & when I get out, I remember I left my wallet. The cab driver just drives away. I go inside my house where I find my wife in bed with the gardener. I leave my home, come to this bar, & just when I was thinking about putting an end to my life, you show up & drink my poison."

On hearing that her elderly grandfather has just passed away, Katie goes straight to her grandparents' house to visit her 95-year-old grandmother and comfort her. When she asks how her grandfather has died, her grandmother replies, "He had a heart attack while we were making love on Sunday morning." Horrified, Katie tells her grandmother that two people nearly 100 years old having sex will surely be asking for trouble. "Oh no, my dear. Many years ago, realizing our advanced age, we figured out the best time to do it was when the church bells would start to ring. It was just the right rhythm. It was nice, slow, and even. Nothing too strenuous, simply in on the ding and out on the dong." She pauses, wipes away a tear and then continues, "And if that damned ice cream truck hadn't come along, he'd still be alive today!"

I knew a blonde that was so stupid; she put lipstick on her forehead because she wanted to make up her mind.

A wealthy man was having an affair with an Italian woman for a few years. One night, during one of their rendezvous, she confided in him that she was pregnant. Not wanting to ruin his reputation or his marriage, he paid her a large sum of money if she would go to Italy to have the child. If she stayed in Italy, he would also provide child support until the child turned 18. She agreed, but wondered how he would know when the baby was born. To keep it discrete, he told her to mail him a postcard, and write "Spaghetti" on the back. He would then arrange for child support. One day, about 9 months later, he came home to his confused wife. "Honey," she said, "you received a very strange postcard today." "Oh, just give it to me and I'll explain it later," he said. The wife handed the card over and watched as her husband read the card, turned white, and fainted. On the card was written "Spaghetti, Spaghetti, Spaghetti. Two with meatballs, one without."

This is the true story of George Phillips of Meridian, Mississippi, who was going to bed when his wife told him that he'd left the light on in the shed. George opened the door to go turn off the light but saw there were people in the shed in the process of stealing things.
He immediately phoned the police, who asked, "Is

someone in your house?" and George said, "No," and explained the situation. Then they explained that all patrols were busy, and that he should simply lock his door and an officer would be there when available.

George said, "Okay," hung up, counted to 30, and phoned the police again.

"Hello, I just called you a few seconds ago because there were people in my shed. Well, you don't have to worry about them now because I've just shot them all."

Then he hung up. Within five minutes three squad cars, an Armed Response unit, and an ambulance showed up. Of course, the police caught the burglars red-handed.

One of the policemen said to George, "I thought you said that you'd shot them!"

George said, "I thought you said there was nobody available!"

Late one night a burglar broke into a house and while he was sneaking around he heard a voice say, "Jesús is watching you." He looked around and saw nothing. He kept on creeping and again heard, "Jesús is watching you." In a dark corner, he saw a cage with a parrot inside. The burglar asked the parrot, "Was it you who said Jesús is watching me" The parrot replied, "Yes." Relieved, the burglar asked, "What is your name?" The parrot said, "Clarence." The burglar said, "That's a stupid name for a parrot. What idiot named you Clarence?" The parrot answered, "The same idiot that named the rottweiler Jesús."

Politicians and diapers have one thing in common: they should both be changed regularly... and for the same reason.

Three contractors are bidding to fix a broken fence at the White House. One is from Chicago, another is from Tennessee, and the third is from Minnesota. All three go with a White House official to examine the fence. The Minnesota contractor takes out a tape measure and does some measuring, then works some figures with a pencil. "Well," he says, "I figure the job will run about $900. $400 for materials, $400 for my crew, and $100 profit for me." The Tennessee contractor also does some measuring and figuring, and then says, "I can do this job for $700. $300 for materials, $300 for my crew, and $100 profit for me." The Chicago contractor doesn't measure or figure, but leans over to the White House official and whispers, "$2,700." The official, incredulous, says, "You didn't even measure like the other guys! How did you come up with such a high figure?" The Chicago contractor whispers back, "$1000 for me, $1000 for you, and we hire the guy from Tennessee to fix the fence." "Done!" replies the government official. And that, my friends, is how the government works.

Mother superior tells two new nuns that they have to paint their room without getting any paint on their clothes. One nun suggests to the other, "Hey, let's take all our clothes off, fold them up, and lock the door." So they do this, and begin painting their room. Soon they hear a knock at the door. They ask, "Who is it?" "Blind man!" The nuns look at each other and one nun says, "He's blind, so he can't see. What could it hurt?" They let him in. The blind man walks in and says, "Hey, nice tits. Where do you want me to hang the blinds?"

A husband says to his wife, "You know, our son got his brain from me." The wife replies, "I think he did. I still got mine with me!"

Mickey Mouse is in the middle of a nasty divorce from Minnie Mouse. Mickey spoke to the judge about the separation. "I'm sorry Mickey, but I can't legally separate you two on the grounds that Minnie is mentally insane," said the judge. Mickey replied, "I didn't say she was mentally insane, I said that she's fucking Goofy!"

I named my hard drive "dat ass," so once a month my computer asks if I want to "back dat ass up."

Q: What kind of bees make milk instead of honey?
A: Boo-bees

Q: What do you call a pig that does karate?
A: A pork chop.

There is a senior citizen driving on the highway. His wife calls him on his cell phone and in a worried voice says, "Herman, be careful! I just heard on the radio that there is a madman driving the wrong way on Route 280!" Herman says, "I know, but there isn't just one, there are hundreds!"

Everyone says the world would be better off if it was run by women. Sure, maybe there wouldn't be violence and territorial conquests fueled by male testosterone. But instead, we'd have a bunch of jealous countries that aren't talking to each other.

I saw a young teenage kid on the subway today. He had a Mohawk hairstyle dyed yellow, green, and red. He caught me staring at him and in a nasty voice asked, "What the f*ck are you looking at?" I replied, "Sorry, but when I was about your age I had sex with a parrot. I thought maybe you were my son."

THREE TREES AND A WOODPECKER
Two tall trees, a birch and a beech, are growing in the woods. A small tree begins to grow between them, and the beech says to the birch, "Is that a son of a beech or a son of a birch?" The birch says he cannot tell, but just then a woodpecker lands on the sapling.
The birch says, "Woodpecker, you are a tree expert. Can you tell if that is a son of a beech or a son of a birch?"
The woodpecker takes a taste of the small tree and replies, "It is neither a son of a beech nor a son of a birch, It is, however, the best piece of ash I have ever poked my

pecker into."
Now wipe that smile off your face.

A man is sitting at a bar enjoying a cocktail when an exceptionally gorgeous, sexy, young woman enters. The man can't stop staring at her. The young woman notices this and walks directly toward him. Before he could offer his apologies for being so rude, the young woman says to him, "I'll do anything you want me to do, no matter how kinky, for $100, with one condition." Flabbergasted, the man asks what the condition is. The young woman replies, "You have to tell me what you want me to do in just three words." The man considers her proposition for a moment, withdraws his wallet from his pocket, and hands the woman five $20 bills. He looks deeply into her eyes and slowly says, "Paint my house."

What do a pizza boy and a gynecologist have in common? They both smell it but they can't eat it.

Yo momma is so black; she got marked absent at night school.

A man boards a plane with six kids. After they get settled in their seats, a woman sitting across the aisle leans over to him and asks, "Are all of those kids yours?" He replies, "No. I work for a condom company. These are customer complaints."

An old teacher asked her student, "If I say, 'I am beautiful,' which tense is that?" The student replied, "It is obviously past."

Yo mama so fat I tried driving around her and I ran out of gas.

A husband and wife were driving through Louisiana. As they approached Natchitoches, they started arguing about the pronunciation of the town. They argued back and forth, and then they stopped for lunch. At the counter, the husband asked the blonde waitress, "Before we order, could you please settle an argument for us? Would you please pronounce where we are very slowly?" She leaned over the counter and said, "Burrr-gerrr Kiiing."

A blonde's neighbor's house was on fire so she called 911. The blonde told the operator, "My neighbor's house is on fire!" The operator asked, "Where are you?" The blonde answered, "At my house." The operator replied, "No, I'm asking how we get there?" The blonde said, "In a fire truck, duh!"

How do you get a one handed blonde down from a tree? Wave at her.

How do you know when a woman is about to say something smart? When she starts her sentence with, "A man once told me..."

Q: What do you call a stupid Chinese prostitute?
A: Wun Dum Ho.

Three guys and a lady were sitting at the bar talking about their professions. The first guy says, "I'm a YUPPIE. You know, young, urban, professional." The second guy says, "I'm a DINK. You know, double income, no kids." The third guy says, "I'm a RUB. You know, rich urban biker." They turn to the woman and ask, "So what are you?" The woman replies, "I'm a WIFE. You know - Wash, Iron, Fuck, Etc."

How are women and tornadoes alike? They both moan like hell when they come, and take the house when they leave.

A bus full of ugly people had a head on collision with a truck. When they died, God granted all of them one wish. The first person said, "I want to be gorgeous." God snapped his fingers and it happened. The second person said the same thing and God did the same thing. This went on and on throughout the group. God noticed the last man in line was laughing hysterically. By the time God got to the last ten people, the last man was laughing and rolling on the ground. When the man's turn came, he laughed and said, "I wish they were all ugly again."

Q: Have you heard about McDonald's new Obama Value Meal?
A: Order anything you like and the guy behind you has to pay for it.

Yo momma's so fat; her baby pictures were taken by satellite.

Q: Why did only 1,800 Mexicans show up to the Battle of the Alamo?
A: They only had two vans.

Q: What's the only positive thing about living in the ghetto?
A: Pregnancy tests.

A boy asks his mom, "Why am I black and you're white?" She says, "Don't even go there. The way that party went, you're lucky you don't bark."

Q: What does the receptionist at the sperm clinic say when clients are leaving?
A: "Thanks for coming!"

Q: What did the penis say to the condom?
A: "Cover me. I'm going in."

Dad: "Say 'daddy.'"
Baby: "Mommy!"
Dad: "Come on, say 'daddy!'"
Baby: "Mommy!"
Dad: "Fuck you. Say 'daddy!'"
Baby: "Fuck you. Mommy!"
Mom: "Honey, I'm home!"
Baby: "Fuck you!"
Mom: "Who taught you to say that?"
Baby: "Daddy!"
Dad: "Son of a bitch."

How did the blonde try to kill the bird?? She threw it off a cliff.

China, Russia, and Poland venture to space. China says they'll go to Pluto because it's the farthest. Russia says they'll go to Jupiter because it's the biggest. Poland says they'll go to the Sun. Russia and China warn that they'll melt. They reply, "We'll go at night."

They say that during sex you burn off as many calories as running 8 miles. Who the hell runs 8 miles in 30 seconds?

A 3 years old boy sits near a pregnant woman.
Boy: Why do you look so fat?
Pregnant woman: I have a baby inside me.
Boy: Is it a good baby?
Pregnant woman: Yes, it is a very good baby.
Boy: Then why did you eat it?!

A blonde gets lost and calls for directions. The operator asks which cross streets she's at. The blonde replies, "I'm on the corner of Walk and Do Not Walk."

Why did the women cross the road? I don't know, but what is she doing out of the kitchen?

A boy is selling fish on a corner. To get his customers' attention, he is yelling, "Dam fish for sale! Get your dam fish here!" A pastor hears this and asks, "Why are you calling them 'dam fish.'" The boy responds, "Because I caught these fish at the local dam." The pastor buys a couple fish, takes them home to his wife, and asks her to cook the dam fish. The wife responds surprised, "I didn't know it was acceptable for a preacher to speak that way." He explains to her why they are dam fish. Later at the dinner table, he asks his son to pass the dam fish. He responds, "That's the spirit, Dad! Now pass the fucking potatoes!"

On their way to get married, a young Catholic couple is involved in a fatal car accident. The couple found themselves sitting outside the Pearly Gates waiting for St. Peter to process them into Heaven. While waiting, they began to wonder: Could they possibly get married in Heaven? When St. Peter showed up, they asked him. St. Peter said, "I don't know. This is the first time anyone has asked. Let me go find out,'" and he left. The couple sat and waited, and waited. Two months passed and the couple was still waiting. While waiting, they began to wonder what would happen if it didn't work out; could you get a divorce in heaven? After yet another month, St. Peter finally returned, looking somewhat bedraggled. "Yes," he informed the couple, "You can get married in Heaven." "Great!" said the couple, "But we were just wondering, what if things don't work out? Could we also get a divorce in Heaven?" St. Peter, red-faced with anger, slammed his clipboard onto the ground. "What's wrong?" asked the frightened couple. "OH, COME ON!," St. Peter shouted, "It took me three months to find a priest up here! Do you have any idea how long it'll take me to find a lawyer?"

Why don't witches wear panties? So they can get a better grip on the broom!

Yo momma's so fat, her measurements are 36-24-26, and that's just her left arm.

A blonde, a fat brunette, and a skinny redhead find a magic mirror. If you lie to the mirror you die. The redhead says, "I look fat," and dies. The brunette says, "I look skinny," and dies. The blonde says, "I think..." and dies.

What happens if a Jew with an erection walks face first into a wall? He breaks his nose.

Student: "Should I get in trouble for something I didn't do?"
Teacher: "No."
Student: "Good, because I didn't do my homework."

Yo momma's so ugly, the government moved Halloween to her birthday!

Why do women wear panties with flowers on them? In loving memory of all the faces that have been buried there.

Q: What do black people and sperm have in common?
A: Only one in a million work.

Grandma and Grandpa were visiting their kids overnight. When Grandpa found a bottle of Viagra in his son's medicine cabinet, he asked about using one of the pills. The son said, "I don't think you should take one Dad, they're very strong and very expensive." "How much?" asked Grandpa. "$10.00 a pill," answered the son. "I don't care," said Grandpa, "I'd still like to try one, and before we leave in the morning, I'll put the money under the pillow."

Later the next morning, the son found $110 under the pillow. He called Grandpa and said, "I told you each pill was $10, not $110."I know," said Grandpa. "The hundred is from Grandma!"

A mom of an eight year old boy is awaiting her son's arrival from school. As he runs in, he says he needs to talk to her about making babies. He claims he knows about the development of a fetus, but doesn't understand the answer to the million dollar question. Namely, how does the sperm get into the woman? The mom asks the boy what he thinks the answer is. The boy says that the sperm is manufactured in the man's stomach, rises up to his chest, then throat, and into his mouth, where he then kisses the woman and deposits the sperm into her mouth. The mom tells her boy that it is a good guess, but it's wrong. She gives him a hint by telling him that the sperm comes out of the man's penis. Suddenly, the boy's face becomes quite red and he says, "You mean you put your mouth on that thing?"

What do you call two Mexicans playing basketball? Juan on Juan.

Yo momma's so ugly; her birth certificate is an apology letter from the condom factory.

You know you're getting fat when you say you're fat in front of your friends and nobody corrects you.

Yo momma's so ugly she makes the blind go crippled!

Q: Why does Humpty Dumpty love autumn?
A: Because Humpty Dumpty had a great fall.

Yo momma is so fat she went to church with heels on and when she came back home they were flats.

Yo Momma's teeth are so yellow, that when she smiles, traffic slows down!

A blonde, a brunette, and a redhead all work at the same office for a female boss who always goes home early. "Hey girls," says the brunette, "Let's go home early tomorrow. She'll never know." The next day, they all leave right after the boss does. The brunette gets some extra gardening done, the redhead goes to a bar, and the blonde goes home to find her husband having sex with the female boss! She quietly sneaks out of the house and returns at her normal time. "That was fun," says the brunette. "We should do it again sometime." "No way," says the blonde. "I almost got caught!"

One day in the forest, 3 guys were just hiking along a trail when all of a sudden; a huge pack of Indians attacked them and knocked them out. When they woke up, they were at the leader of the tribe's throne. The chief then said, "All of your lives may be spared if you can find ten of one fruit and bring them back to me." So after a while the first man returned with 10 apples. The chief then ordered him to stick all ten of them up his butt without making any expression at all on his face. He had a little bit of trouble with the first one and started crying while trying to put the next one in. He was soon killed. Later, the next guy came in with 10 grapes. The chief soon ordered him to do the same as the first guy. After to the 9th grape, the man started laughing so hard for no apparent reason, and was killed. The first two guys soon met in heaven and the first guy asked the second, "Why did you start laughing? You only needed one more grape and you'd have gotten away!" The second guy answered while still laughing, "I couldn't help it. I saw the third guy walking in with pineapples."

Q: Did you hear about the kidnapping at school?
A: It's okay. He woke up.

Two mental patients were walking next to a swimming pool. One jumped into the pool and the other jumped in to save him. Their doctor saw the rescue and called the rescuer to his office. "Due to your actions, it appears your mental state is fine," the doctor said to the patient, "You can go home to your family, but before you do, you should know that the person you saved hung himself today." The patient replied, "He didn't hang himself; I hung him there to dry."

There was an elderly couple who in their old age noticed that they were getting a lot more forgetful, so they decided to go to the doctor. The doctor told them that they should start writing things down so they don't forget. They went home and the old lady told her husband to get her a bowl of ice cream. "You might want to write it down," she said. The husband said, "No, I can remember that you want a bowl of ice cream." She then told her husband she wanted a bowl of ice cream with whipped cream. "Write it down," she told him, and again he said, "No, no, I can remember: you want a bowl of ice cream with whipped cream." Then the old lady said she wants a bowl of ice cream with whipped cream and a cherry on top. "Write it down," she told her husband and again he said, "No, I got it. You want a bowl of ice cream with whipped cream and a cherry on top." So he goes to get the ice cream and spends an unusually long time in the kitchen, over 30 minutes. He comes out to his wife and hands her a plate of eggs and bacon. The old wife stares at the plate for a moment, then looks at her husband and asks, "Where's the toast?"

An explorer goes into an undiscovered tomb for the first time, and in the center of the tomb there's a lamp. He picks it up, and as he starts to rub the dirt off of it, a genie comes out of the lamp and says, "I want to know the person you hate the most." The explorer says, "That's gotta be my ex-wife. Why?" "I am a cursed genie. I will grant you three wishes, but whatever you wish for, your ex-wife will get double that amount." "Okay, I wish for a billion dollars." "Granted, but you ex-wife gets two billion dollars." "I wish for a mansion in California with a swimming pool, and tennis courts, everything." "Granted, and your ex-wife gets two." "Now make your final wish." The explorer walks around for a few minutes, returns to the genie with a stick, and says, "You see this stick? I'd like you to beat me half to death."

Q: What did the green grape say to the purple grape?
A: "Breathe, stupid!"

During the wedding rehearsal, the groom approaches the pastor with an unusual offer. "Look, I'll give you $100 if you'll change the wedding vows. When you get to the part where I'm supposed to promise to 'love, honor, and obey' and 'be faithful to her forever,' I'd appreciate it if you'd just leave that out." He passes the minister a $100 bill and walks away satisfied. On the day of the wedding, when it comes time for the groom's vows, the pastor looks the young man in the eye and says, "Will you promise to prostrate yourself before her, obey her every command and wish, serve her breakfast in bed every morning of your life, and swear eternally before God and your lovely wife that you will not ever even look at another woman, as long as you both shall live?" The groom gulps, looks around, and says in a tiny voice, "Yes," then leans toward the pastor and hisses, "I thought we had a deal." The pastor puts a $100 bill into the groom's hand and whispers, "She made me a better offer."

A husband got his mother-in-law a cemetery plot for Christmas. It came with a coffin, tomb stone, the works.

Next Christmas comes by and the husband gets her nothing. When the mother-in-law asks, "Why didn't you get me a gift?" the husband says, "You haven't used the one I got you last year!"

A doctor reaches into his smock to get a pen to write a prescription and pulls out a rectal thermometer. "Oh, damn it," he proclaims, "Some asshole has my pen!"

Two Jews walk into a bar and ask for some water. Why? Because it's free.

What do you call an African-American whose spouse just died? A black widow.

How come it takes so long to build a blonde snowman? Because you have to hollow out the head.

Q: What is Mozart doing right now?
A: Decomposing.

Man: I want to give myself to you.
Woman: Sorry, I don't accept cheap gifts.

Q: Why are black people so good at basketball?
A: They are good at running, stealing, and shooting.

Yo mamma so stupid she tried to put M&M's in alphabetical order.

One day Little Johnny asks his mom, "How come when I come in to your room you and you're on top of Daddy, you say you're making a sandwich, but after a while I come in again, you're eating a sausage?!"

Yo momma so stupid she stuck a phone up her butt and thought she was making a booty call!

A husband, who has six children, begins to call his wife "mother of six" rather than by her first name. The wife, amused at first, chuckles. A few years down the road, the wife has grown tired of this. "Mother of six," he would say, "what's for dinner tonight? Get me a beer!" She gets very frustrated. Finally, while attending a party with her husband, he jokingly yells out, "Mother of six, I think it's time to go!" The wife immediately shouts back, "I'll be right with you, father of four!"

A Mexican, a Cuban, and a Chinese guy are riding in a truck. Who's driving? Immigration.

A teacher asked, "Johnny, can you tell me the name of three great kings who have brought happiness and peace into people's lives?" Little Johnny responded, "Drin-king, smo-king, and fuc-king."

A blonde walks into a shoe store and tries on a pair of shoes. "How do they feel?" asks the salesclerk. "Well, they feel a bit tight," replies the blonde. The assistant promptly bends down and has a look at the shoes and the blonde's feet. "Try pulling the tongue out," offers the clerk. "Nath, theyth sthill feelth a bith tighth," the blonde replies.

Teacher: "What is the chemical formula for water?"
Student: "HIJKLMNO."
Teacher: "What are you talking about?"
Student: "Yesterday you said it's H to O!"

One weekend, a husband is in the bathroom shaving when the local kid Bubba he hired to mow his lawn, comes in to pee. The husband slyly looks over and is shocked at how immensely endowed Bubba is. He can't help himself, and asks Bubba what his secret is. "Well," says Bubba, "every night before I climb into bed with a girl, I whack my penis on the bedpost three times. It works, and it sure impresses the girls!" The husband was excited at this easy suggestion and decided to try it that very night. So before climbing into bed with his wife, he took out his penis and whacked it three times on the bedpost. His wife, half-asleep, said, "Bubba? Is that you?"

What's the difference between three penises and a joke?
Your mom can't take a joke.

Jill goes home one night with a guy she met at a club. He's tall, super hot, and seems different than most guys she meets. They arrive at his place and head straight to his room. Jill can't help but notice a shelf full of teddy bears. On the bottom are small teddy bears, on the middle are medium-sized teddy bears, and finally, on the top are large teddy bears, all lined up beside each other. She begins to think that he is sentimental and sweet, and isn't afraid to show it. Her heart melts and she want to give him the best night of his life. She gives him a blowjob, and lets him really give it to her, and even takes it in the rear! In the morning, she slowly gets dressed, and smiles at him and asks, "How was that?" He nods and says, "Not too fuckin' bad at all. Help yourself to a prize on the second shelf!"

Q: What's the difference between a black and an Asian?
A: 10 minutes in the oven.

One woman I was dating called and said, "Come on over, there's nobody home." I went over. Nobody was home.

A blonde is wearing a pair of socks that don't match, one is red and the other is white. Her friend sees her out and says, "You know your socks don't match, right? You're wearing one red sock and one white sock." The blonde responds, "That's so weird! I have another pair just like it in my drawer at home."

Yo momma is so ugly her momma had to tie a steak around her neck to get the dog to lick her.

An old man is met by his attorney, and is told he is going to be audited. He rides to the IRS office with his attorney, and when he gets there, he begins to talk with the IRS agent. "I bet $2,000 I can bite my own eye!" The IRS agent agrees to the bet, believing it an impossible task. The old man laughs, pulls out his glass eye, and bites it. The IRS agent is dumbfounded. The old man bets $3,000 he can bite his other eye. The IRS agent knows there's no way possible to do this, so he once more agrees. The old man cackles, pulls out his dentures, and bites his eye. Then the old man finally wagers, "I bet $20,000 I can stand on the far side of your desk, pee over the desk, and get it into your wastebasket, without missing a single drop." The agent knows he won't be able to, so once more he agrees. The old man indeed misses, peeing all over the desk, and on the paperwork. The IRS agent jumps for joy, but then notices the attorney over in the corner moaning. "Are you all right?" asks the agent. "No! On the way over here, he bet me $400,000 he could pee on your desk and you'd be happy about it!"

There are five cows on a farm, one mamma cow and four baby calves. The first baby walks up to the mom and asks,

"Momma, why is my name Rose?" The mommy cow replies, "Well honey, a rose petal fell on your head when you were born." The next calf comes up and asks, "Momma, why is my name Lily?" The mother replies, "Because honey, a lily petal fell on your head when you were born." The third baby comes up and asks, "Momma, why is my name Daisy?" The momma cow again replies" Well, when you were born a daisy petal fell on your head." The final baby walks over and says, "Duh huh guh nuh!" The momma cow says, "Shut up, Cinderblock."

If at first you don't succeed, skydiving is not for you!

A police officer sees a blonde woman driving and knitting at the same time. Exasperated, he drives up next to her and screams out the window, "Pull over!" The blonde responds, "No Silly, it's a scarf."

A group of fathers are sitting around talking about their teenage daughters. One dad says, "I think my 16 year old is smoking; I found an empty cigarette pack under her bed." All the other fathers say in unison, "Oh no!" Then a second dad says, "That's nothing. I found an empty liquor bottle under my 16 year old's bed." All the other fathers say in unison, "Oh dear!" Then a third dad says, "Mine's worse than both of those combined: I went into my 16 year old daughter's room and found a used condom." All the other fathers say in unison, "Jesus Christ!" The third father replies "Yeah, I didn't know she had a dick!"

What's six inches long, two inches wide, and drives women wild? Money.

Sherlock Holmes and Dr. Watson went on a camping trip. After a good meal and a bottle of wine, they lay down for the night, and went to sleep. Some hours later, Holmes awoke and nudged his faithful friend. "Watson, look up at the sky and tell me what you see." Watson replied, "I see millions and millions of stars." "What does that tell you?" Watson pondered for a minute. "Astronomically, it tells me that there are millions of galaxies, and potentially billions of planets. Astrologically, I observe that Saturn is in Leo. Horologic ally, I deduce that the time is approximately a quarter past three. Theologically, I can see that God is all powerful and that we are small and insignificant. Meteorologically, I suspect that we will have a beautiful day tomorrow. What does it tell you?" Holmes was silent for a minute, and then spoke. "It tells me that someone has stolen our tent."

There's an elderly couple who has reached that point in life, where sex isn't part of the itinerary anymore. One night, the wife turns to her husband and says, "Every time one of us wants to have a bit of a slap and tickle, we just have to say, "Washing machine.'" A night passes, and the husband leans over and whispers, "Washing machine." The wife gives him a shove and informs him that she has a headache. A few nights go by and the same thing happens, but the husband is determined and he reckons he'll just give it one more try. He leans over and whispers seductively, "Washing machine." Yet again, the wife turns him away. However, a few moments pass and the wife's needs arises so she rolls over and recites the word, but the husband turns over and says, "Sorry love, it was only a small wash so I did it by hand."

A professor was giving a lecture on involuntary muscular contractions to his first year medical students. Realizing that this was not the most riveting subject, he decided to lighten the mood. He pointed to a young woman in the front row and asked, "Do you know what your asshole is doing while you're having an orgasm?" She replied, "He's probably playing golf with his friends."

Yo mom is so dumb that she thought Dunkin' Donuts was a basketball team.

A bus full of housewives going on a picnic crashed with no survivors. Each husband cried for a week, but one husband continued for more than two weeks. When asked he replied miserably, "My wife missed the bus."

Q: What do you call a bench full of white people?
A: The NHL.

How many snowboarders does it take to screw in a light bulb? 50: 3 to die trying, 1 to actually pull it off, and 46 other to say, "Man, I could do that!"

Got tasered picking up my friend from the airport today. Apparently security doesn't like it when you shout, "Hi Jack!"

Yo momma's so fat, she wakes up in sections.

A husband asks his wife, "Will you marry after I die?" The wife responds, "No, I will live with my sister." The wife asks him back, "Will you marry after I die?" The husband responds, "No, I will also live with your sister."

A man walks by a blonde, who is holding a pig. The man asks, "Where did you get her?" The pig answered, "I won her at the fair."

A man joins a soccer team and his new teammates inform him, "At your first team dinner as the new guy, you will have to give us a talk about sex." The evening arrives and he gives a detailed, humorous account of his sex life. When he got home, his wife asked how the evening went and not wanting to lie, but also not wanting to explain exactly what happened, he said, "Oh, I had to make a talk about yachting," his wife thought this a little peculiar but said nothing more and went to sleep. The next day she bumped into one of his new teammates at the supermarket and asked, "I heard my husband had to make a speech last night. How did it go?" His mate said smiling, 'Oh, it was excellent! Your husband is clearly very experienced!." The wife looked confused and replied to his mate, "Strange, he has only done it twice and the second time he was sick."

Q: What is the difference between Tiger Woods and Santa Claus?
A: Santa stops after three hos.

Golfer: "I'd move heaven & earth to break 100 on this course." Caddy: "Try heaven; you've already moved most of the earth."

A Giants fan, a Padre fan, and a Dodger fan are climbing a mountain and arguing about who loves his team more. The Padre fan insists he's the most loyal. "This is for San Diego!" he yells and jumps off the side of the mountain. Not to be outdone, the Giants fan is next to profess his love for his team. He yells, "This is for San Francisco!" and pushes the Dodger fan off the mountain.

A woman was nagging her husband to cut the grass, to which the husband answered, "What do I look like to you? A landscaper?!" Next time the sink was dripping, she asked him again, "Honey, can you fix the faucet?" The husband replied, "What do I look like to you? A Plumber?!" Two days later, a light bulb went out and she begged him again, "Honey, can you change the light bulb?" His reply was, "What am I? An electrician?!" A few days later, the husband comes home from work to find that the lawn is cut, the faucet is fixed, and the light bulb is changed. Very surprised, he says, "Honey, what happened here?" The wife replies, "You know our new next door neighbor? He came over and fixed everything." The husband says, "Honey, how did you pay him?!" "Oh, you know," the wife says, "he told me that I could either bake him a cake or have sex with him." Somewhat relieved the husband asks, "Whew, so what kind of a cake did you bake for him?" The wife replies, "Who do you think I am? Betty Crocker?!"

The huge college freshman decided to try out for the football team. "Can you tackle?" asked the coach. "Watch this," said the freshman, who proceeded to run smack into a telephone pole, shattering it to splinters. "Wow," said the coach. "I'm impressed. Can you run?" "Of course I can run," said the freshman. He was off like a shot, and, in just over nine seconds, he had run a hundred yard dash. "Great!" enthused the coach. "But can you pass a football?" The freshman hesitated for a few seconds. "Well, sir," he said, "If I can swallow it, I can probably pass it."

This blonde calls me and says, "What's your phone number? I can't find it!"

Yo mama so ugly she gives Freddy Krueger nightmares.

What is easier to pick up the heavier it gets? Women.

Why can't you hear rabbits making love? Because they have cotton balls.

When a man opens the car door for his wife, you can be sure of one thing, either the car is new or the wife is.

Teacher: "If I gave you 2 cats and another 2 cats and another 2, how many would you have?"
Johnny: "Seven."
Teacher: "No, listen carefully... If I gave you two cats, and another two cats and another two, how many would you have?"
Johnny: "Seven."
Teacher: "Let me put it to you differently. If I gave you two apples, and another two apples and another two, how many would you have?"
Johnny: "Six."
Teacher: "Good. Now if I gave you two cats, and another two cats and another two, how many would you have?"
Johnny: "Seven!"
Teacher: "Johnny, where in the heck do you get seven from?!"
Johnny: "Because I've already got a freaking cat!"

Johnny was at school and the teacher said, "Someone use fascinate in a sentence." Sally answered, "The zoo was fascinating." The teacher said, "Sorry, Sally, I said to use fascinate in a sentence." Maria suggested, "I was fascinated at the zoo." Once again the teacher said, "No, Maria, I specifically said to use fascinate in a sentence." Johnny said, "My sister has ten buttons on her sweater." Again the teacher said, "Sorry, Johnny, I said use fascinate in a sentence." Johnny replied, "I know, but her boobs are so big she can only fasten eight."

Q: Why is Santa Claus' sack so big? A: He only comes once a year.

Q: Did you hear about the man with a broken left arm and broken left leg?
A: Don't worry he's "ALRIGHT" now!

Wife: "Our new neighbor always kisses his wife when he leaves for work. Why don't you do that?"
Husband: "How can I? I don't even know her."

Three men are traveling on a ship, when they are accosted by the Devil. The Devil proposes that if each man drops something into the sea and he cannot find it, he will be that man's slave. If the Devil does find it, however, he will eat that man up. The first man drops a pure, clear diamond, and immediately gets eaten. The second drops an expensive watch, trying to impress the Devil, and gets eaten. The third man fills a bottle with water and pours it into the sea yelling, "You think I'm a fool? Try finding that!"

A man and a woman are sleeping together when suddenly there is a noise in the house, and the woman rolls over and says, "It's my husband, you have to leave!" The man jumps out of bed, jumps through the window, crawls through the bushes, and out on the street, when he realizes something. He goes back to the house and says to the woman, "Wait, I'm your husband!" She replies giving him a dirty look, "So why did you run?"

A Sunday school teacher asked her children on the way to service, "And why is it necessary to be quiet in church?" One little girl replied, "Because people are sleeping."

How many cops does it take to arrest a Mexican? Eight. One to carry him, the rest to carry his oranges.

A man who is just married is flying to the Florida Keys for a business trip. His new bride is to accompany him the next day. When he gets there, he e-mails his wife to let her know he made it there safely. When he sends the e-mail, he mistypes the address. In Boston, a grieving widow, whose husband has recently passed away, receives the e-mail. She reads it, screams, and faints. Hearing her grandmother's cry, the widow's 18 year old granddaughter runs into the living room to see the computer on, with a message that reads, "Dear love, I just got here. Preparing for your arrival tomorrow. Can't wait to see you. Love, Me. P.S. Sure is hot down here."

Q: What's the difference between a black man and Batman?
A: Batman can go inside a store without Robin.

A blonde, brunette, and redhead are all on a building about to jump off. They all jump at the same time. Which one landed last? The blonde because she asked for directions.

You are so ugly; the last time you got a piece of ass was when your hand slipped through the toilet paper.

Q: When can women make you a millionaire? A: When you're a billionaire.

A father passing by his son's bed room was astonished to see the bed was nicely made, and everything was picked up. Then, he saw an envelope, propped up prominently on the pillow. It was addressed, "Dad." With the worst premonition, he opened the envelope and read the letter, with trembling hands...
"Dear, Dad. It is with great regret and sorrow that I'm writing you. I had to elope with my new girlfriend, because I wanted to avoid a scene with mom and you.
I've been finding real passion with Stacy, and she is so

nice, but I knew you would not approve of her because of her piercings, tattoos, tight motorcycle clothes, and because she is so much older than I am.

But it's not only the passion, Dad. She's pregnant. Stacy said that we will be very happy. She owns a trailer in the woods, and has a stack of firewood for the whole winter. We share a dream of having many more children.

Stacy has opened my eyes to the fact that marijuana doesn't really hurt anyone. We'll be growing it for ourselves, and trading it with the other people in the commune, for all the cocaine and ecstasy we want. In the meantime, we'll pray that science will find a cure for AIDS, so Stacy can get better. She sure deserves it!

Don't worry, Dad. I'm 15, and I know how to take care of myself. Someday, I'm sure we'll be back to visit, so you can get to know your many grandchildren.

Love, your son, Joshua.

P.S. Dad, none of the above is true. I'm over at Jason's house. I just wanted to remind you that there are worse things in life than the school report card that's on the kitchen table. Call when it is safe for me to come home!

What's the difference between an Irish wedding and an Irish wake? One less drunk Irishman.

Did you hear about the guy who died of a Viagra overdose? They couldn't close his casket.

A man driving a car hits a woman. Whose fault is it? The man's. Why was he driving in the kitchen?

I went to the bank the other day and asked the banker to check my balance, so she pushed me!

Q: What do computers eat for a snack?
A: Microchips!

An old man takes his grandson fishing in a local pond one day. After 20 minutes of fishing, the old man fires up a cigar. The young boy asks, "Grandpa, can I have a cigar?" The old man asks, "Son, can your dick touch your asshole?" The young boy says no. "Then u can't have a cigar." Another 20 minutes passes, and the old man opens a beer. The young boy asks, "Grandpa, can I have a beer?" The old man asks, "Son, can your dick touch your asshole?" The young boy says no. "Well, then u can't have a beer." Another 20 minutes passes and the young boy opens a bag of potato chips. The old man asks, "Son, can I have some of your chips?" The boy asks, "Well, Grandpa, can your dick touch your asshole?" The old man says, "It sure can." The boy says, "Well good, then go fuck yourself, these are my chips."

A chicken walks into a library, goes up to a librarian and says, "Book book book." The librarian decides that the chicken wants a book so he gives the chicken a book and the chicken walks away. About ten minutes later the chicken comes back with the book, looking a bit agitated, saying, "Book book book." The librarian decides the chicken wants another book so he takes the old book back and gives the chicken another book. The chicken walks out the door. Ten minutes later the chicken comes back again, very agitated, saying, "Book book book!" so quickly it almost sounds like one word. The chicken puts the book on the librarian's desk and looks up - waiting for another book. This time the librarian gives the chicken another book and decides that something weird is happening. He follows the chicken out the door and into the park, all the way to the pond. In the pond is a frog sitting on a lily pad. The chicken gives the book to the frog, who then says, "Reddit, reddit."

Little Johnny likes to gamble. One day, his dad gets a new job, so his family has to move to a new city. Johnny's dad thinks, "I'll get a head start on Johnny's gambling." He calls the teacher and says, "My son Johnny will be starting your class tomorrow, but he likes to gamble, so you'll have to keep an eye on him." The teacher says, "Okay," because she can handle it. The next day, Johnny walks into class and hands the teacher an apple and says, "Hi, my name is Johnny." She says, "Yes, I know who you are." Johnny smiles and says, "I bet you $10 you've got a mole on your butt." The teacher thinks that she will break his little gambling problem, so she takes him up on the bet. She pulls her pants down, shows him her butt, and there is no mole. That afternoon, Johnny goes home and tells his dad that he lost $10 to the teacher and explains why. His dad calls the teacher and says, "Johnny said that he bet you that you had a mole on your butt and he lost." The teacher says, "Yeah, and I think I broke his gambling problem." Johnny's dad laughs and says, "No you didn't, he bet me

$100 this morning that he'd see your ass before the day was over."

Why did the Mexican guy throw his wife off of a cliff? Tequila!

A blonde sees a thermos in a store. She asks a clerk, "What is that and what's it for?" The clerk answers, "It's a thermos that keeps hot things hot and cold things cold." The blonde says, "I'll take it." When she gets to work, her blonde boss asks, "What is that?" The blonde worker says, "It's a thermos. It keeps cold things cold and hot things hot." "Whatcha got in it?" "A cup of coffee and a Popsicle."

The Penis Study. The American Government funded a study to see why the head of a man's penis was larger than the shaft. After one year and $180,000, they concluded that the reason that the head was larger than the shaft was to give the man more pleasure during sex. After the US published the study, the French decided to do their own study. After $250,000 and three years of research, they concluded that the reason the head was larger than the shaft was to give the woman more pleasure during sex. Canadians, unsatisfied with these findings, conducted their own study. After two weeks and a cost of around $75.46, and two cases of beer, they concluded that it was to keep a man's hand from flying off and hitting himself in the forehead.

If you ever get cold, just stand in the corner of a room for a while. They're normally around 90 degrees.

Man: "Wanna hear a joke about my penis? Oh never mind, it's too long."
Woman: "Want to hear a joke about my vagina? Never mind, you'll never get it."

A man hasn't been feeling well, so he goes to his doctor for a complete checkup. Afterward, the doctor comes out with the results. "I'm afraid I have some very bad news," the doctor says. "You're dying, and you don't have much time left." "Oh, that's terrible!" says the man. "How long have I got?" "Ten," the doctor says sadly. "Ten?" the man asks. "Ten what? Months? Weeks? What?!" "Nine..."

Your Halloween costume came in the mail today. I opened it. It was a rooster mask and a bag of lollipops. Going as a cock sucker again!?

Yo mama so stupid, she got hit by a parked car.

A blonde woman decides that she is sick and tired of all the blonde jokes and how all blondes are perceived as stupid, so she decides to show her husband that blondes really are smart. While her husband is off at work, she decides that she is going to paint a couple of rooms in the house. The next day, right after her husband leaves for work, she gets down to the task at hand. Her husband arrives home at 5:30 and smells the distinctive smell of paint. He walks into the living room and finds his wife lying on the floor in a pool of sweat. He notices that she is wearing a ski jacket and a fur coat at the same time. He goes over and asks her if she is OK. She replies yes. He asks what she is doing. She replies that she wanted to prove to him that not all blonde women are dumb and she wanted to do it by painting the house. He then asks her why she has a ski jacket over her fur coat. She replies that she was reading the directions on the paint can and they said, "For best results, put on two coats."

A friend of mine got in trouble for punching an african-american woman. In his defense, he was told to go to Home Depot and get a black and decker

A little boy wants a bike for Christmas really badly, but the kid is a real bad seed, and he knows it. He writes a letter to Jesus. "Dear Jesus, if I get a bike for Christmas, I'll be good for a whole week." He thinks about it, crosses out what he wrote, and says, "I can't be good for a whole week, I'll be good for five days." He crosses that out and writes, "I'll be good for four days." Then he thinks again and says, "Can't do that." He gets down to one day and says, "I can't even be good for a day." Then in frustration, goes in his mother's room and get the statue of the Virgin Mary, wraps it up in a blanket, puts it in a paper bag, throws it in the closet and says, "Dear Jesus, if I don't get a bike for Christmas, you'll never see your mother again!"

An old man goes to a church, and is making a confession:
Man: "Father, I am 75 years old. I have been married for 50 years. All these years I had been faithful to my wife, but yesterday I was intimate with an 18 year old."
Father: "When was the last time you made a confession?"
Man: "I never have, I am Jewish."
Father: "Then why are telling me all this?"
Man: "I'm telling everybody!"

Two friends die. One goes to Heaven and the other goes to Hell. The one that goes to Heaven begs the angel to let him visit his friend in Hell, and the angel agrees. He gets to Hell and sees his friend surrounded by beautiful women and alcohol everywhere. He says to his friend, "Wow, you were a son of a bitch when we were alive! Hell looks better than Heaven." So the friend in Hell says, "Pour yourself a glass of wine." The heavenly friend pours the wine, and notices that the glass has no bottom. The good friend looks at the bad one in confusion, and the bad friend says, "The glass has no bottom, and neither do the girls. Welcome to Hell."

How do you kill a blonde? Put a scratch and sniff sticker at the bottom of a swimming pool.

Why is Santa Claus so jolly? Because he knows where all the naughty girls live.

Yo momma's like a postal stamp: lick it, stick it, and then send that bitch away.

Alfie was listening to his sister practice her singing. "Sis," he said, "I wish you'd sing Christmas carols." "That's nice of you, Alfie," she replied, "but why?" Alfie replied, "Because then I'd only have to hear your voice once a year!"

Three old timers at the retirement home were complaining about growing old. The first one says, "I wake up at 7:00 AM and try for a half hour to take a poop." The second one says, "Oh yeah? I spend an hour trying to pee." The third one says, "I take a nice poop at 7:00 AM and about 7:30 AM take a nice pee." The other two guys look at him and ask, "What are you complaining about?" The third man explains, "I don't wake up till 8:30 AM."

Your momma is so stupid she put airbags on her computer in case it crashed.

A Spanish captain was walking on his ship when a soldier rushes to him and exclaims, "An enemy ship is approaching us!" The captain replies calmly, "Go get my red shirt." The soldier gets the shirt for the captain. The enemy ship comes in and heavy rounds of fire are exchanged. Finally, the Spaniards win. The soldier asks, "Congrats sir, but why the red shirt?" The captain replies, "If I got injured, my blood shouldn't be seen, as I didn't want my men to lose hope." Just then, another soldier runs up and says, "Sir, we just spotted another twenty enemy ships!" The captain calmly replies, "Go bring my yellow pants."

A man asks his wife, "What would you do if I won the lottery?" His wife says, "Take half and leave your ass!" The man replies, "Great! I won 12 bucks, here is six, now get out!"

Why did God create men? Because vibrators can't mow the lawn.

Little Susie, a six-year-old, complained, "Mother, I've got a stomach ache." "That's because your stomach is empty," the mother replied. "You would feel better if you had something in it." That afternoon, her father came complaining that he had a severe headache all day. Susie perked up, "That's because it's empty," she said. "You'd feel better if you had something in it."

A young boy comes home from school in a bad mood. His father asks him, "What's wrong, son?" The kid tells his dad that he's upset because another kid has been teasing him and calling him gay. The father says, "Punch him in the face next time he does that. I bet he'll stop." The kid replies, "Yeah, but he's so cute!"

A drunk walks into a bar with jumper cables around his neck. The bartender says, "You can stay but don't try to start anything."

One day a blonde went into the library and asked the librarian, "Can I have a burger and fries?" The librarian replied, "This is the library." Then blonde whispered, "Oh sorry. Can I have a burger and fries?"

A married man was having an affair with his secretary. One day, their passions overcame them in the office and they took off for her house. Exhausted from the afternoon's activities, they fell asleep and awoke at around 8 p.m. As the man threw on his clothes, he told the woman to take his shoes outside and rub them through the grass and dirt. Confused, she nonetheless complied and he slipped into his shoes and drove home. "Where have you been?" demanded his wife when he entered the house. "Darling," replied the man, "I can't lie to you. I've been having an affair with my secretary. I fell asleep in her bed and didn't wake up until eight o'clock." The wife glanced down at his shoes and said, "You liar! You've been playing golf!"

A magician worked on a cruise ship in the Caribbean. The audience would be different each week, so the magician did the same tricks each week. However, there was a problem, the captain's parrot saw the shows each week and began to understand how the magician did every trick. Once he understood, he started shouting out the secrets in the middle of the show, "Look, it's not the same hat." "Look, he is hiding the flowers under the table." "Hey, why are all the cards the Ace of Spades?" The magician was furious but couldn't do anything; it was, after all, the captain's parrot. One day, the ship had an accident and sank. The magician found himself with the parrot, adrift on a piece of wood, in the middle of the ocean. They stared at each other with hatred, but did not utter a word. This went on for a day, then another, and another. Finally, after a week, the parrot said, "Okay, I give up. Where the heck is the boat?"

A kid from Mississippi is on Harvard campus for the first time, he stops a student and asks, "Excuse me, can you tell me where the library is at?" The Harvard student replies "At Harvard, you don't end a sentence with a preposition." The kid said, "Sorry about that. Can you tell me where the library is at, asshole?"

Three nuns are talking. The first nun says, "I was cleaning in Father's room the other day and do you know what I found? A bunch of pornographic magazines." "What did you do?" the other nun asks. "Well, of course I threw them in the trash." The second nun says, "Well, I can top that. I was in Father's room putting away the laundry and I found a bunch of condoms!" "Oh my!" gasp the other nuns. "What did you do?" they ask. "I poked holes in all of them!" she replies. The third nun faints.

Why is it that your nose runs, but your feet smell?

I was wondering why the ball kept getting bigger and bigger, and then it hit me.

A young man and woman got married. At the time of their marriage, the husband noticed his wife carried a decently sized metal box and shoved it up at the top of their closet. Curious as he was, the wife told him to never to look in it no matter what the circumstances. Over the years, he saw that metal box in the closet, but never peered into it for the sake of his wife. One day, though, the wife had a stroke and was rushed to the hospital. As the husband sat grieving at home, he thought of the box, snatched it up, and sped to the hospital where his wife remained with her death coming soon. The husband bolted to her hospital room and pleaded and begged her to allow him to open the box by her side. "Well" she said, "I suppose now would be the right time." The husband unlatched the hook and peered inside. On one side sat two crocheted dolls, and on the other, to his surprise, sat one million dollars! "Honey, before we got married, my mother gave me this box and told me that whenever I got mad at you, I should go to the bedroom and crotchet a doll," said the wife. The husband was thrilled and thankful. He absolutely couldn't believe his wife had only been mad at him two times! "That is amazing!" said the husband to his wife. "Honey, I'm grateful beyond belief you've only been mad at me twice, but how on this earth did you manage to get one million dollars?" "Oh, honey" said the wife, "That's the money I got from selling the dolls."

Dad: "Can I see your report card, son?"
Son: "I don't have it."
Dad: "Why?"
Son: "I gave it to my friend. He wanted to scare his parents."

Yo momma is so ugly that when the Kool-Aid man broke through her wall he said, "Oh noooo!"

What do you do when 50 zombies surround your house? Hope its Halloween.

Four gay guys are sitting in a Jacuzzi when all of a sudden, a condom starts floating. One of the gay guys turns around and asks, "Okay, who farted?"

Yo mama so black that when she jumped into the pool it turned into coffee.

One night a lady came home from her weekly prayer meeting, found she was being robbed, and she shouted out, "Acts 2:38: 'Repent & be baptized & your sins will be forgiven.'" The robber quickly gave up & the lady rang the police. While handcuffing the criminal, a policeman said, "Gee mate, you gave up pretty easily. How come you gave up so quickly?" The robber said, "She said she had an axe and two 38's!"

Interviewer: "What's your greatest weakness?"
Candidate: "Honesty."
Interviewer: "I don't think honesty is a weakness."
Candidate: "I don't give a fuck what you think."

A guy's talking to a girl in a bar.
He asks her, "What's your name?"
She says, "Carmen."
He says, "That's a nice name. Who named you, your mother?"
She says, "No, I named myself."
He says, "Why Carmen?"
She says, "Because I like cars and I like men. What's your name?"
He says, "Beerfuck."

Yo momma's so stupid, she steals samples from stores!

How do you get an Iranian out of a bathtub? You turn on the water.

Men have two emotions, hungry and horny. If you see him without an erection, make him a sandwich.

A little girl is serving her father tea while her mother is out shopping. The mother comes home and the father says, "Watch this!" The little girl goes and serves the mother tea. The mother responds, "Did it ever occur to you that the only place she can reach to get water is the toilet?"

Yo mama so dumb she tried to make an appointment with Dr. Pepper.

An old lady went to visit her dentist. When it was her turn, she sat in the chair, lowered her underpants, and raised her legs. The dentist said, "Excuse me, but I'm not a gynecologist." "I know," said the old lady. "I want you to take my husband's teeth out."

A couple is trying to have a baby. Finally, the blonde tells her husband, "Honey, I have great news! We're pregnant, and we're having twins!" The husband is overjoyed and says to his wife, "Honey that's wonderful, but how do you know so soon that we're having twins?" She nods her head and says, "Well, I bought the twin pack pregnancy test and they both came out positive!"

Scientists have discovered a food that diminishes a woman's sex drive by 90%. It's called a wedding cake.

My friend asked me, "Why are you getting a divorce?" I responded, "My wife wasn't home the entire night and in the morning she said she spent the night at her sister's house." He said, "So?" And I responded, "She's lying. I spent the night at her sister's house!"

Q: What did the Mexican say when the house fell on him?
A: "Get off me, homes!"

A man gets on a bus, and ends up sitting next to a very attractive nun. Enamored with her, he asks if he can have sex with her. Naturally, she says no, and gets off the bus. The man goes to the bus driver and asks him if he knows of a way for him to have sex with the nun. "Well," says the bus driver, "every night at 8 o'clock, she goes to the cemetery to pray. If you dress up as God, I'm sure you could convince her to have sex with you." The man decides to try it, and dresses up in his best God costume. At eight, he sees the nun and appears before her. "Oh, God!" she exclaims. "Take me with you!" The man tells the nun that she must first have sex with him to prove her loyalty. The nun says yes, but tells him she prefers anal sex. Before you know it, they're getting down to it, having nasty, grunty, loud sex. After it's over, the man pulls off his God disguise. "Ha, ha!" he says, "I'm the man from the bus!" "Ha, ha!" says the nun, removing her costume, "I'm the bus driver!"

Why did the bald man cut a hole in his pocket? He wanted to run his fingers through his hair.

What do you call it when a blonde dyes her hair brunette? Artificial intelligence.

A young man goes into a drug store to buy condoms. The pharmacist tells him that the condoms come in packs of three, nine, or 12, and asks which ones the young man wants. "Well," he says, "I've been seeing this girl for a while and she's really hot. I want the condoms because I think tonight's the night. We're having dinner with her parents and then we're going out. Once she's had me, she'll want me all the time, so you'd better give me the 12 pack!" The young man makes his purchase and leaves. Later that evening, he sits down to dinner with his girlfriend and her parents. He asks if he may give the blessing and they agree. He begins the prayer, but continues praying for several minutes. The girl leans over and says, "You never told me that you were such a religious person." He leans over to her and says, "You never told me that your father is a pharmacist."

A blonde goes into a computer store and asks the clerk, "Where do you keep the curtains for computers?" The clerk answers with a puzzled face, "Curtains for computers? You don't need curtains for computers." The blonde's eyes widen and she shakes her head as she answers, "Hello!?? My computer has Windows!!"

Yo mama so stupid, she returned a donut because it had a hole in it.

A super hot chick walks into her church and says to the priest, "Forgive me Father, for I have sinned." The priest says, "Tell me dear, what's on your mind?" "Well Father, I am a sex addict, and lately I discovered that I like doing it with priests. I had sex with the one from the church two blocks from here, the one five blocks from here, and also the one from the church nearby." The priest says, "Its okay, just pray three times a day for one week and it will all be okay." As the girl tries to go out, the priest says, "Oh, and don't forget that I will always be here for you!"

How many men does it take to open a beer? None. It should be opened by the time she brings it.

Yo momma's so fat, when she went to the beach, the whales sang, "We are family!"

A man and his wife go to their honeymoon hotel for their 25th anniversary. As the couple reflected on that magical evening 25 years ago, the wife asked the husband, "When you first saw my naked body in front of you, what was going through your mind?" The husband replied, "All I wanted to do was to fuck your brains out, and suck your tits dry." Then, as the wife undressed, she asked, "What are you thinking now?" He replied, "It looks as if I did a pretty good job."

A taxi passenger taps the driver on the shoulder to ask him a question. The driver screams, loses control of the car, nearly hits a bus, goes up on the footpath, and stops centimeters from a shop window. For a second, everything goes quiet in the cab, then the driver says, "Look mate, don't ever do that again. You scared the daylights out of me!" The passenger apologizes and says, "I didn't realize that a little tap would scare you so much." The driver replies, "Sorry, it's not really your fault. Today is my first day as a cab driver. I've been driving a funeral van for the last 25 years."

Yo momma so dumb when I said "Drinks on the house," she got a ladder.

Q: What nails do carpenters hate to hit?
A: Fingernails.

Yo mama is so fat on Halloween she threw on a white sheet and went as Antarctica.

A man walks into a doctor's office. The doctor examines the man and then gives him his diagnosis. Doctor: "You'll live to be 60!"
Patient: "I am 60!"
Doctor: "See! What did I tell you?"

Did you hear what happened to the blonde ice hockey team? They drowned in spring training.

A man came home from work, sat down in his favorite chair, turned on the TV, and said to his wife, "Quick, bring me a beer before it starts" She looked a little puzzled, but brought him a beer. When he finished it, he said, "Quick, bring me another beer. It's gonna start." This time she looked a little angry, but brought him a beer. When it was gone, he said, "Quick, another beer before it starts." "That's it!" She blows her top, "You bastard! You waltz in here, flop your fat ass down, don't even say hello to me and then expect me to run around like your slave. Don't you realize that I cook and clean and wash and iron all day long?" The husband sighed. "Oh shit, it started!"

A man speaks frantically into the phone, "My wife is pregnant, and her contractions are only two minutes apart!" "Is this her first child?" the doctor queries. "No, you idiot!" the man shouts. "This is her husband!"

Three women (a blonde, a redhead, and a brunette) are lost in the forest while hunting. They each have a shotgun with 2 bullets. They make a fire. Then the redhead gets up and goes hunting. She comes back with 2 rabbits. The other two say, "Wow, where did you get that?" She says, "I found tracks. I followed tracks. I saw rabbits. Rabbits ran. I shot. Rabbits stopped." Then the brunette leaves and comes back with a deer. The other two say, "Wow, Where did you get that?" She says, "I found tracks. I followed tracks. I saw deer. Deer ran. I shot. Deer stopped." The blonde leaves and comes crawling back, all bloodied and black and blue. They others say, "Wow, where did you get that?" She says, "I found tracks. I followed tracks. I saw train. Train ran. I shot. Train didn't stop."

Yo mama's so fat, when she steps on a scale, it says, "Please step out of the car."

I never forget a face! But in your case I'll make an exception!

A doctor tells an old couple at his office he needs to get a stool sample, a urine sample, and a blood test from the old man. Hard of hearing, the old man asks his wife what the doctor said. The wife replies, "He needs a pair of your underwear."

Q: What do you do when a blonde throws a grenade at you?
A: Pull the pin and throw it back.
Q: What do you do when a blonde throws a pin at you?
A: Run because she has a grenade in her mouth.

Your momma is so old her breasts are full of powdered milk.

At the doctor's office, Tom was getting a checkup. "I have good news and bad news," says the doctor. "The good news is you have 24 hours left to live." Tom replies, "That's the good news?!" Then the doctor says, "The bad news is I should have told you that yesterday."

A boy with a monkey on his shoulder was walking down the road when he passed a policeman who said, "Now, now young lad, I think you had better take that monkey the zoo." The next day, the boy was walking down the road with the monkey on his shoulder again, when he passed the same policeman. The policeman said, "Hey there, I thought I told you to take that money to the zoo!" The boy answered, "I did! Today I'm taking him to the cinema."

A wife asked her husband, "Honey, will you still love me when I am old and overweight?" The man replied, "Yes, I do."

A Polish man, a German guy, and an American dude, climb a mountain because they each want to make a wish from the genie on the top. When they make it to the top, they find the lamp and all rub it. The genie appears and says, "For your wish to be granted, you must yell it out while you are jumping off of this mountain." So the German jumps off and yells, "I wish to be a fighter plane!" "So be it," the genie says, and the German becomes a plane. The American jumps off and yells, "I wish to be an eagle!" "So be it," the genie says, and the American becomes an eagle and flies away. The Polish man runs to the edge, accidentally trips on a rock, and yells, "I wish to b- oh Shit!"

Two buddies were sharing drinks while discussing their wives. "Do you and your wife ever do it doggie style?" asked the one. "Well, not exactly." His friend replied, "She's more into the trick dog aspect of it." "Oh, I see, kinky, huh?" "Well, not exactly. I sit up and beg, and she rolls over and plays dead."

Three guys are at the gates of Heaven, and God tells them, "We have a special today! If you died a terrible death, you're in for free." So God asks the first guy his story. "I was a hard working man and a loving husband, but I began to suspect that my wife was cheating on me. One day, I called in sick to work and left for home to hide and closely watch my apartment. I saw a man go in, and I decided to wait a few minutes to catch them in the act. Then, I started banging on my door. They wouldn't open it, so I broke down the door and walked in to see my wife sitting naked, but the man wasn't in sight. I went to the balcony, where I saw a naked man hanging on the edge. I began to stomp on his hands until he fell down, but there were bushes, so I got my fridge and tossed it on him. In the process of tossing the fridge, I also fell over and died." God replies, "Wow, that's pretty bad, finding out your wife cheated and falling off your balcony. You pass." The second guy says, "God, my only crime was that I enjoyed dancing naked in my apartment while eating pickles out of the jar. I was doing just that one day, when I slipped on a pickle and fell over my balcony. Luckily, I was able to grab on to the ledge below mine. After a few minutes, a man came and I thought he was going to rescue me, but he began to stomp on my hands. I fell, but luckily, I fell into the bushes. I thought I had survived, but that man threw a fridge at me and I died!" God replies, "Wow, that's very cruel, being crushed to death." The third man says, "I died naked in a fridge."

A woman had never seen Santa Claus before, but on Christmas Eve night she heard someone come down her chimney so she went downstairs to check it out. "Oh, it's Santa Claus," she said, "Please stay and chat this is the first time I have met you." Santa replied, "Ho ho ho, I need to go. I need to go!" The lady took off her robe, but Santa said, "Ho ho ho, I need to go. I need to go!" The lady slipped off her nightgown and Santa told her, "Ho ho ho, I need to go. I need to go!" Then the lady removed her panties, and Santa said, "Hey hey hey, I need to stay. I need to stay, 'cause I can't go up the chimney with my dick this way!"

Gandhi walked barefoot most of the time, which produced an impressive set of calluses on his feet. He also ate very little, which made him rather frail and with his odd diet, he suffered from bad breath. This made him a super calloused fragile mystic hexed by halitosis.

If you think nobody cares if you're alive, try missing a couple of car payments.

A kid walks up to his mom and asks, "Mom, can I go bungee jumping?" The mom says "No, you were born from broken rubber and I don't want you to go out the same way!"

A woman is at a grocery store. She goes to the clerk to purchase her groceries. The clerk looks at her items and sees a carton of eggs, a gallon of milk, and a head of lettuce. He says to the woman, "You must be single." The woman was surprised & replies, "Yes, how did you know?" The clerk answers, "Because you're ugly."

There was a blonde driving in the country side when she went around the corner and saw an ocean of wheat fields. Then she saw a blonde in a row boat frantically paddling. The blonde driver yelled out, "Hey! It's blondes like you that give blondes like me a bad name and if I knew how to swim, I'd swim out there and kick your ass!"

So this dude comes home from work one day, and his wife is watching the Food Network. The husband asks, "Why do you watch that? You still can't cook," and the wife responds, "Why do you watch porn? You still can't fuck."

A blonde goes to a soda machine in a casino. She puts in a dollar and gets a soda. She does this again and again. A man in line behind her asks why she is taking so long. She says, "Can't you see I'm winning?"

I'm a mailman. At Christmas this year, Mrs. Jankowitz met me at the door and invited me in for a great breakfast spread. After I ate, I thanked her and she said, "There's more." She took me to her bedroom and showed me moves I had never imagined. I told her I had no idea she felt this way. She said, "I don't." I ask, "What was all this about?" She says, "I asked the husband what to give the mailman." He said, "Screw the mailman, breakfast was my idea."

Being Asian and a woman definitely has its advantages. For example, when you've had a few drinks and have to drive home past midnight, you think you're driving perfectly fine, but in reality you're not. Next thing you know, there's a cop. The cop sees you and doesn't even bother pulling you over, let alone giving you a ticket. Why? Well, he's probably thinking, "This person's not under the influence, it's just an Asian woman driving!"

Yo mama's so poor that ducks throw bread at her.

Q: What did one tampon say to the other? A: Nothing, they were both stuck up bitches.

A man asks a woman, "Haven't I seen you someplace before?" The woman responds, "Yeah, that's why I don't go there anymore."

Q: Why shouldn't you make fun of a paleontologist?
A: Because you will get Jurasskicked.

How do you embarrass an archaeologist? Show him a used tampon and ask, "What period is this from?"

If you eat too much Chinese food you will get two chins .... And a chang.

Bernie was invited to his friend's home for dinner. Morris, the host, preceded every request to his wife by endearing terms, calling her Honey, My Love, Darling, Sweetheart, Pumpkin, etc. Bernie looked at Morris and remarked, "That's really nice, that after all these years that you have been married, and you keep calling your wife those pet names." Morris hung his head and whispered, "To tell you the truth, I forgot her name three years ago!"

Q: Why do pilgrim's pants fall down?
A: Because their belts are on their hats.

There was an elderly man who wanted to make his younger wife pregnant. He went to the doctor to get a sperm count. The doctor told him to take a specimen cup home, fill it, and bring it back. The elderly man came back the next day; the specimen cup was empty and the lid was on it. The doctor asked, "What was the problem?" The elderly man said, "Well, I tried with my right hand... nothing. I tried with my left hand... nothing. So my wife tried with her right hand... nothing. Her left hand... nothing. Her mouth... nothing. Then my wife's friend tried. Right hand, left hand, mouth... still nothing. The doctor replied, "Wait a minute, did you say your wife's friend too?!" The elderly man answered, "Yeah, and we still couldn't get the lid off of the specimen cup."

A priest, a minister, and a rabbi want to see who's best at his job. So they each go into the woods, find a bear, and attempt to convert it. Later they get together. The priest begins: "When I found the bear, I read to him from the Catechism and sprinkled him with holy water. Next week is his first communion." "I found a bear by the stream," says the minister, "and preached God's holy word. The bear was so mesmerized that he let me baptize him." They both look down at the rabbi, who is lying on a gurney in a body cast. "Looking back," he says, "maybe I shouldn't have started with the circumcision."

Q: How can you get a blonde to laugh on Saturday?
A: Tell her a joke on Wednesday.

Q: Why didn't the man report his stolen credit card?
A: The thief was spending less than his wife.

A young woman asked her mom if she could go out for some fries and eat them with friends for 2 hours. Her mom said, "Sure." However, the daughter went to her boyfriends and had sex with him for 2 hours. When she came back home, her mom asked her how the fries were. The daughter replied, "Nice!" The mom said, "I can tell you enjoyed them; there's still mayonnaise dripping from your face."

I don't really like watching basketball; I just watch it to find out who the next member of the Kardashian family will be.

Little Johnny was at school and heard the word "bitch." He asks his mom what the word meant and she responds, "It means priest." The next day little Johnny hears the word "shit" and asks his dad what it means. His dad answers, "It means food." At school, he hears the word "fucking" and asks his mom what it means. She responds, "It means getting ready." The next day a priest came over for dinner and little Johnny opened the door and says, "Hey bitch.

There's shit on the table and my parents are upstairs fucking!"

A woman goes to a doctor named Dr. Wong. "Doctor, I can't get a date, no one will go out with me." In a very thick Asian accent, Dr. Wong says, "Take off clothes and get on all four hands and knees." She does. "Now crawl to wall." She does so and looks back at him. "I know what wrong." "What is it Doctor! What do I have?" "You have Ed Zachary disease." "Ed Zachary disease? What is that?!" "You face look Ed Zachary like you ass!"

Why did the blonde jump off the cliff? She thought her maxi pad had wings.

I want to die peacefully in my sleep, like my grandfather. Not screaming and yelling like the passengers in his car.

Q: What did the black boy say when he had diarrhea?
A: "Mommy, why am I melting?!"

Q: What did Obi-Wan say to Luke at the breakfast table?
A: "Use the fork, Luke."

A blonde was swerving all over the road and driving very badly, so she got pulled over by a cop. The cop walked up to her window and asked, "Miss, why are you driving so recklessly?" The blonde said, "I'm sorry sir, but wherever I go, there's always a tree in front of me and I can't seem to get away from it!" The cop looked at her and said, "Ma'am, that's your air freshener!"

How do you fix a woman's watch? You don't. There is a clock on the oven.

What do you call a German virgin? Goodandtight.

Three blondes had boyfriends all named John and they kept getting confused. They decided to name them after sodas. The first girl said, "I'll call mine 7 Up, because he's seven inches and he's always up." The next girl said, "I'll call mine Mountain Dew, because he mounts me and knows exactly what to do." The last girl goes, "I'll call mine Jack Daniels." The other girls yelled at her and said, "That's not a soda! That's a hard licker!"

An old lady was getting on the bus to go to the pet cemetery with her cat's remains. As she got on the bus, she whispered to the bus driver, "I have a dead pussy." The driver pointed to the lady sitting behind him and said, "Sit with my wife, you two have a lot in common."

A man walks into a bar and orders a shot, and then he looks into his shirt pocket and orders another one. After he finishes, he looks into his pocket again and orders another shot. The bartender is curious and asks the man why he looks into his pocket before ordering each shot. The man replies, "I have a picture of my wife in my pocket, and when she starts to look good, I go home."

Yo momma's so fat, when she gets in an elevator, it has to go down.

Yo mama so dark when I clicked on her profile pic, I thought my phone died.

A guy believed that his wife is cheating on him, so he hired a private investigator. The cheapest he could find was a Chinese man. This was the Chinese PI's report about what he found: "*Most honorable, sir. You leave house. I watch house. He come to house. I watch. He and she leave house. I follow. He and she go in hotel. I climb tree. I look in window. He kiss she. He strip she. She strip he. He play with she. She play with he. I play with me. I fall out tree. I not see. No fee. Cheng Lee.*"

A man calls 911 and says, "I think my wife is dead." The operator says, "How do you know?" The man says, "The sex is about the same, but the ironing is piling up!"

Why do men die before their wives? They want to.

In surgery for a heart attack, a middle-aged woman has a vision of God by her bedside. "Will I die?" she asks. God says, "No. You have 30 more years to live." With 30 years to look forward to, she decides to make the best of it. So since she's in the hospital, she gets breast implants, liposuction, a tummy tuck, hair transplants, and collagen injections in her lips. She looks great! The day she's discharged, she exits the hospital with a swagger, crosses the street, and is immediately hit by an ambulance and killed. Up in heaven, she sees God. "You said I had 30 more years to live," she complains. "That's true," says God. "So what happened?" she asks. God shrugs, "I didn't recognize you."

too crispy, not too burnt, but right in the groove. And while you're at it, throw in a shake, not too thin, not too thick, but right in groove." The waiter took down the order and came back five minutes later and told the man, "The cook said you can kiss his ass, not to the left, not to the right, but right in the groove."

An old man goes into the Social Security Office and fills out an application. Too old to have a birth certificate, he is asked to prove he is old enough. He opens his shirt and shows them the gray hair on his chest and they accept that as proof. He goes home to his wife, shows her the check, and explains to her what has happened. She replies, "Well get back down there, pull down your pants, and see if you can get disability!"

A guy walks into a bathroom, sits down, and notices three buttons in front of him marked, WW, WA, and ATR. Curiosity gets the better of him so he decides to press WW. Suddenly, warm water sprays up his rear. "Mmmm," he says to himself. "That was good." So he presses WA and a jet of warm air dries his backside. "Mmmm. Nice!" So finally he can't resist pressing the ATR button. The next thing he knows, he is waking up in a hospital ward just as the nurse is entering the room. "Nurse, Nurse! Where am I? What happened?" The nurse replies, "You must have missed the sign to not press the ATR button." "What does ATR mean exactly?" says the guy. "Automatic Tampon Remover. Your testicles are under your pillow."

Q: Why did the blonde put water on her computer?
A: To wash the Windows.

Don't be racist; racism is a crime; and crime is for black people.

Three men were at a bar discussing coincidences. The first man said, "My wife was reading <u>A Tale of Two Cities</u> and she gave birth to twins." "That's funny," the second man remarked, "My wife was reading <u>The Three Musketeers</u> and she gave birth to triplets." The third man shouted, "Oh my, I have to rush home!" When asked what the problem was, he exclaimed, "When I left the house, my wife was reading <u>Ali Baba and the Forty Thieves</u>!"

Why is Christmas just like a day at the office? You do all the work and the fat guy with the suit gets all the credit.

A man needed a horse, so he went to a temple and got one. Before he left, the priest told him that it was a special horse. In order to make the horse go, you say, "Thank God," and for it to stop you say, "Amen." So the man left, and a few minutes later he dozed off on his horse. Hours later, he woke up and his horse was racing him towards the edge of a cliff. Just in time, he shouted "Amen!" and the horse stopped a few inches from the edge. "Whew," said the man, "thank God!"

Two hunters are out in the forest when one of them collapses. He doesn't seem to be breathing and his eyes are glazed. The other guy takes out his phone and calls 911 and gasps, "My friend is dead! What can I do?" The operator says "Calm down. I can help. First, let's make sure he's dead." There is a silence, and then a gunshot is heard. Back on the phone, the guy says "OK, now what?"

One day in class, the teacher brought a bag full of fruit and said, "Now class, I'm going to reach into the bag and describe a piece of fruit and you tell me which fruit I'm talking about. Alright, the first one is round, plump, and red. Little Johnny raised his hand high but the teacher ignored him and picked Deborah who promptly answered, "Apple." The teacher replied, "No Deborah, it's a beet, but I like your thinking. Now the second one is soft, fuzzy and colored red and brown." Johnny is hopping up and down in his seat trying to get the teacher to call on him but she calls on Billy. "Is it a peach?" Billy asks. "No, it's a potato, but I like your thinking," the teacher replies. "Okay the next one is long, yellow, and fairly hard." Johnny is about to explode as he waves his hand frantically but the teacher calls on Sally who say, "A banana." The teacher responds, "No, it's a squash, but I like your thinking." Johnny is irritated now so he speaks up loudly, "Hey, I've got one for you teacher. Let me put my hand in my pocket. Okay, I've got it. Its round, hard, and it's got a head on it." "Johnny!" she cries, "That's disgusting!" "Nope," answers Johnny, "It's a quarter, but I like your thinking!"

A husband and wife have four boys. The odd part of it is that the older three have red hair, light skin, and are tall, while the youngest son has black hair, dark eyes, and is short. The father eventually takes ill and is lying on his deathbed when he turns to his wife and says, "Honey, before I die, be completely honest with me. Is our youngest son my child?" The wife replies, "I swear on everything that's holy that he is your son." With that, the husband passes away. The wife then mutters, "Thank God he didn't ask about the other three."

At a wedding party recently, someone yelled, "All the married men please stand next to the one person who has made your life worth living!" The bartender was crushed to death.

If Mary had Jesus, and Jesus is the Lamb of God, does that mean Mary had a little lamb?

Two homeless men are devising a plan to get free drinks at a bar. The first one has an idea: "We'll buy a hot dog and stick it down your pants, walk into the bar, get our drinks, drink, and when the bartender asks for his money, you pull down your pants and I suck on the hot dog that you put down there. He'll kick us out, and we won't have to pay. It's brilliant!" The second man agrees and they do this in the first bar where it works just as planned. Then they hit up 4 more bars and the first man says, "This is great, getting all these free drinks!" The other man replies, "Yeah, especially because the hot dog fell out at the first bar."

On a windy day, an old lady is standing on a street corner, holding on to her hat with both hands, even though her dress is flying up over her face. An old man across the street sees her and runs over. As he approaches her, he says, "Sister, you ought to be ashamed of yourself, standing over here in all this wind with your dress flying over your head, exposing your paraphernalia, and you're holding that damn hat with both hands. You ought to be ashamed." She looked at him and said, "Look here, fool, everything down there is 80 years old, but this hat is brand new."

You're so fat you're the reason why the Earth is tilted.

Yo mamma so fat when she died she broke the stairway to Heaven.

Why is a blonde girl staring at the orange juice box? The orange juice box says, "Concentrated."

Teacher: "Name a bird with wings but can't fly."
Student: "A dead bird, sir."

Q: What do you call a Mexican that lost his car?
A: Carlos.

A man is fishing and he catches a crocodile. The crocodile tells him, "Please let me go! I'll grant you any wish you desire." The man says, "Okay, I wish my penis could touch the ground." The crocodile then bites his legs off.

A funeral service was being held for a young woman who had just passed away. As the pallbearers carried the casket out, they accidentally bumped into a wall. They heard a faint moan come from inside the casket. They opened the casket and found that the woman was still alive! She went on to live 10 more years and then died, and they held another funeral for her. While the pallbearers were carrying her out, her husband yelled, "Watch out for that wall!"

Yo mamma is so fat; black holes get sucked into her.

Q: What's the best thing about Switzerland?
A: I don't know, but the flag is a big plus.

A gentleman is preparing to board a plane, when he hears that the Pope is on the same flight. "This is exciting," thinks the gentleman. "Perhaps I'll be able to see him in person." Imagine his surprise when the Pope sits down in the seat next to him. Shortly after take-off, the Pope begins a crossword puzzle. Almost immediately, the Pope turns to the gentleman and says, "Excuse me, but do you know a four letter word referring to a woman that ends in 'unt?'" Only one word leaps to mind. "My goodness," thinks the gentleman, "I can't tell the Pope that. There must be another word." The gentleman thinks for quite a while, and then it hits him. Turning to the Pope, the gentleman says, "I think the word you're looking for is 'aunt.'" "Of course," says the Pope. "Do you have an eraser?"

What is the difference between jelly and jam? You can't jelly your dick in a vagina.

What do you call a masturbating bull? Beef strokinoff.

The blonde walks into a drugstore and asks the pharmacist for some bottom deodorant. The pharmacist, a little bemused, explains to the woman that they don't sell anything called bottom deodorant, and never have. Unfazed, the blonde assures him that she has been buying the stuff from this store on a regular basis, and would like some more. "I'm sorry," says the pharmacist, "we don't have any."
"But I always get it here," says the blonde.
"Do you have the container it comes in?"
"Yes!" says the blonde, "I will go and get it."
She returns with the container and hands it to the pharmacist, who looks at it and says to her, "This is just a normal stick of underarm deodorant."
The annoyed blonde snatches the container back and

reads out loud from the container: "To apply, push up bottom."

A man goes to a strip club with an alligator. He says, "I bet you that I can put my dick into this alligator's mouth for 1 minute, and when I take it out, it will not be damaged. If I succeed, all of you will buy me drinks. If I fail, I will buy all of you drinks." The other men agree and he puts his dick into the alligator's mouth for 1 minute. After 1 minute, he hits the alligator on the head with a beer bottle, and he opens his mouth. To everyone's surprise, his dick is unharmed. "Now, before you buy me drinks, does anybody else want to try?" After a while, someone in the back finally raises their hand. It's a woman. "I guess I can try," she says, "but you have to promise not to hit me on the head with a beer bottle."

A policeman pulls a man over for speeding and asks him to get out of the car. After looking the man over the policeman says, "Sir, I couldn't help but notice your eyes are bloodshot. Have you been drinking?" The man gets really indignant and says, "Officer, I couldn't help but notice your eyes are glazed. Have you been eating doughnuts?"

Two guys were playing golf. On the tee, Jack hit his shot way left of the fairway in some buttercups. Bob proceeded to hit and his ball went way off to the right in the bushes. Jack eventually found his ball and proceeded to hit in the buttercups. All of a sudden, he heard a big *POOF* and a fairy appeared. She proceeded to say to Jack that she was

Mother Nature and that she was really upset at him for damaging the buttercups. She said, "Jack, for all the damage that you did to my buttercups, you will not have any butter to put on your toast in the morning for the next month. No, as a matter of fact, I am so upset at you that you won't have any butter for the whole next year! That should teach you a lesson so you won't hurt my creations." *POOF* She disappeared. Jack, stunned by what just happened, called out, "Bob! Bob! Come over here quick!" Bob replied, "Wait a sec. I'm hitting my shot and I'll be right over." Jack yelled back at Bob, "Where are you?" Bob answered, "I'm over here in the pussy willows." Jack shouted back, "Don't swing Bob! For the love of God, don't swing!"

A man tells his wife, "Honey, your mom fell down the stairs 15 minutes ago." The wife yells at him, "Why are you just telling me now?" He said, "Because I couldn't stop laughing."

Yo mama so fat she got arrested for carrying 10 pounds of crack.

When someone yawns, do deaf people think they're screaming?

This young fellow is about to be married, and is asking his grandfather about sex. He asks how often you should have it. His grandfather tells him, "When you first get married, you want it all the time, and maybe you'll do it several times a day. Later on, sex tapers off, and you have it once a week or so. Then as you get older, you have sex maybe once a month. When you get really old, you are lucky to have it once a year, like maybe on your anniversary." The young fellow then asks his grandfather, "Well how about you and grandma now?" His grandfather replies, "Oh, we just have oral sex now." "What's oral sex?" The young fellow asks. "Well, she goes to bed in her bedroom, and I go to bed in my bedroom. She yells, 'Screw you,' and I holler back, 'Screw you too!'"

A ventriloquist is performing with his dummy on his lap. He's telling a dumb blonde joke when a young platinum-haired beauty jumps to her feet. "What gives you the right to stereotype blondes that way?" she demands. "What does hair color have to do with my worth as a human being?" Flustered, the ventriloquist begins to stammer out an apology. "You keep out of this!" she yells. "I'm talking to that little jerk on your knee!"

Yo momma is so fat you need to take two trains and a bus just to get on her good side.

One day at school, little Jimmy needed to go to the restroom so he raised his hand. The strict substitute teacher asked him to say the full alphabet before she would let him go. "But Miss, I am bursting to go," said Jimmy. "You may go, but after you say the full alphabet." "A-B-C-D-E-F-G-H-I-J-K-L-M-N-O-Q-R-S-T-U-V-W-X-Y-Z," he said. Catching his mistake, the substitute asked, "Jimmy, where is the 'P?'" He answered, "Halfway down my legs, Miss."

One day, a blonde went to the doctor with both sides of her face burned. The doctor asked, "What happened?" The blonde said, "Well, I was ironing my husband's shirt until the phone rang. I picked it up and half my face was burnt!" The doctor replied, "What about the other half?" The blonde answered, "They called back."

A husband and wife are in church. The preacher notices that the husband has fallen asleep and says to the wife, "Wake your husband up!" The wife answers, "You're the one who made him fall asleep, you wake him up!"

Little Billy came home from school to see the family's pet rooster dead in the front yard. Rigor mortis had set in and it was flat on its back with its legs in the air. When his Dad came home, Billy mentioned, "Dad, our rooster is dead and his legs are sticking in the air. Why are his legs like that?" His father, thinking quickly, said, "Son, that's so God can reach down from the clouds and lift the rooster straight up to heaven." "Gee Dad, that's great," said little Billy. A few days later, when Dad came home from work, Billy rushed out to meet him yelling, "Dad! Dad, we almost lost Mom today!" "What do you mean?" asked his father. "Well Dad, I got home from school early today and went up to your bedroom and there was Mom, flat on her back with her legs in the air, screaming, 'Jesus, I'm coming! I'm coming!' If it hadn't of been for Uncle George holding her down, we'd have lost her for sure!"

Doris is sitting in a bar and says to her friend that she wants to have plastic surgery to enlarge her breasts. The bartender tells her, "Hey, you don't need surgery to do that. I know how to do it without surgery." Doris asks, "How do I do it without surgery?" "Just rub toilet paper between them." Fascinated, Doris says, "How does that make them bigger?" "I don't know, but it sure worked for your ass!"

A man drinks a shot of whiskey every night before bed. After years of this, the wife wants him to quit. She gets two shot glasses, fills one with water and the other with whiskey. After bringing him to the table that has the glasses, she brings his bait box. She says, "I want you to see this." She puts a worm in the water, and it swims around. She puts a worm in the whiskey, and the worm dies immediately. She then says, feeling that she has made her point clear, "What do you have to say about this experiment?" He responds by saying, "If I drink whiskey, I won't get worms!"

Yo momma is so stupid when I told her Christmas is right around the corner she went looking for it.

One day Jimmy got home early from school and his mom asked, "Why are you home so early?" He answered, "Because I was the only one that answered a question in my class." She said, "Wow, my son is a genius. What was the question?" Jimmy replied, "The question was 'Who threw the trash can at the principal's head?'"

Your mamma's so fat people jog around her for exercise.

Four blondes are ordering a few rounds of drinks. Each time they get up, they toast and say, "14 weeks," then they down their drinks. The bartender finally asks the blondes, "What's the deal?" One blonde says, "Well, we bought a boxed puzzle. It said 'two to six years,' and we did it in 14 weeks!"

Two men broke into a drugstore and stole all the Viagra. The police put out an alert to be on the lookout for the two hardened criminals.

A man and woman were having sex. After they were done, the man asks the woman, "Are you a nurse?" The woman answers, "Yes. How did you know?" The man replies, "Because you took care of me so well." Then the woman asks the man, "Are you an anesthesiologist?" He says proudly, "Yes. How do you know?" The woman answers, "Because I didn't feel a thing."

The old couple had been married for 50 years. They were sitting at the breakfast table one morning when the wife says, 'Just think, fifty years ago we were sitting at this same breakfast table together.' 'I know,' the old man said. 'We were probably sitting here naked as a jaybird, too.' 'Well,' Granny snickered. 'Let's relive some old times.' Where upon, the two stripped to the buff and sat back down at the table. 'You know, honey,' the little old lady breathlessly replied, 'My nipples are as hot for you today as they were fifty years ago.' 'I wouldn't be surprised,' replied Gramps. 'One's in your coffee and the other is in your oatmeal.'

Yo mamma is so stupid, she stopped her car at a stop sign and she's still waiting for it to turn green.

Why did Humpty Dumpty push his girlfriend off the wall? So he could see her crack!

An old man goes into Victoria's Secret and tells the salesperson behind the counter he needs a present for his wife. "See," explains the man, "It is my fiftieth wedding anniversary and I would like to get something pretty to surprise the little lady, if you know what I mean." When he gets home, his wife asks with a scowl on her face, "Where have you been?" "Surprise," says the old man and hands her a sexy tiny teddy. The wife rips it from his hand and takes it to the bathroom to try it on. She struggles to make it fit, but it is two sizes too small. She take a long time in the bathroom and hopes her husband will lose interest and fall asleep because it is getting late into the evening. Finally she emerges from the bathroom with all the lights out. She is completely nude and pretends to model it in front of him. Her husband, still sitting up, squinting to try and see finally says, "For as much money I spent on it, they could have at least ironed out the wrinkles."

Q: How can you tell if a blonde used a computer?
A: There's White-Out all over the screen.

Q: Have you ever had Ethiopian food?
A: Neither have they.

A guy goes to see his doctor, and the doctor says, "Well, I'm afraid you have six weeks to live." The guy says, "Oh damn, well what should I do doctor?" The doctor tells him, "You should take a mud bath once a day for the next six weeks," and the guy asks, "Why? Is that supposed to help?" and the doctor says, "No, but it'll get you used to being in the ground."

Yo momma so stupid, she tried to talk into an envelope to send a voicemail.

A panda walks into a bar, sits down, and orders a sandwich. He eats, pulls out a gun, and shoots the waiter dead. As the panda stands up to go, the bartender shouts,

"Hey! Where are you going? You just shot my waiter and you didn't pay for the food!" The panda yells back, "Hey man, I'm a panda. Look it up!" The bartender opens his dictionary to panda, "A tree climbing mammal of Asian origin, characterized by distinct black and white coloring. Eats, shoots, and leaves."

Marriage is a 3-ring circus: engagement ring, wedding ring, and suffering.

Step 1: Name your iPhone "Titanic."
Step 2: Plug it into your computer.
Step 3: When iTunes says "Titanic is syncing," press cancel.
Step 4: Feel like a hero.

Two women friends had gone out for a girl's night out, and had been overenthusiastic on the cocktails. Incredibly drunk and walking home, they suddenly realized they both needed to pee. They were very close to a graveyard, and one of them suggested they do their business behind a headstone or something. The first woman had nothing to wipe with, so she took off her panties, used them, and threw them away. Her friend however, was wearing an expensive underwear set and didn't want to ruin hers, but was lucky enough to salvage a large ribbon from a wreath that was on a grave and proceeded to wipe herself with it. After finishing, they made their way home. The next day, the first woman's husband phones the other husband and says, "These girls' nights out have got to stop. My wife came home last night without her panties." "That's nothing," said the other. "Mine came back with a sympathy card stuck between the cheeks of her butt that said, "From all of us at the fire station, we'll never forget you!"

What do you call a cow with no legs? Ground beef.

A thief stuck a pistol in a man's ribs and said, "Give me your money." The gentleman, shocked by the sudden attack, said, "You cannot do this, I'm a congressman!" The thief replied, "In that case, give me MY money!"

A blonde goes on a hot date and ends up making out with the guy in his car. The guy asks if she would like to go in the backseat. "No!" yells the blonde. Things get even hotter, and the guy asks again. "For the last time, no!" says the blonde. Frustrated, the guy asks, "Well, why the hell not?" The blonde says, "Because I wanna stay up here with you!"

Q: What's the difference between being hungry and being horny? A: Where you put the cucumber.

Q: What do you do when you drop your phone in water? A: You put it inside a bag of rice which attracts Asians who fix it for you.

A doctor and a lawyer are talking at a party. Their conversation is constantly interrupted by people describing their ailments and asking the doctor for free medical advice. After an hour of this, the exasperated doctor asks the lawyer, "What do you do to stop people from asking you for legal advice when you're out of the office?" "I give it to them," replies the lawyer, "and then I send them a bill." The doctor is shocked, but agrees to give it a try. The next day, still feeling slightly guilty, the doctor prepares the bills. When he goes to place them in his mailbox, he finds a bill from the lawyer.

If women aren't supposed to be in the kitchen, then why do they have milk and eggs inside them?!

Johnny wanted to get his mom something nice for Christmas but she's hard to shop for. Passing a pet store he thought, "Hmm, a pet might be a good idea." He walked in the pet store and asked the manager what might be a good idea. "How about a puppy?" "No," said Johnny. "It may poop around the house." "A fish?" "No, her house is small, so I don't think an aquarium will fit." Johnny then spied a parrot and asked, "How about that parrot?" "Oh," said the manager, "That's Chet. He's very expensive." "Well," said Johnny, "It's my mom let's take a look." The manager went to Chet, put a lighter under his left wing, and Chet started to sing "Jingle bells, jingle bells..." Then the manager put a lighter under Chet's right wing and it started to sing, "Dashing through the snow..." "Wow!" said Johnny, "What else does he sing?" The manager held the lighter under Chet's crotch at which point Chet sang, "Chestnuts roasting on an open fire."

Q: What do you call a skeleton in the closet?
A: The 1863 Blonde Hide-and-Seek champion!

A man is being arrested by a female police officer, who informs him, "Anything you say can and will be held against you." The man replies, "Boobs!"

Q: Why did Barbie never get pregnant?
A: Because Ken came in a different box.

Q: What do dim lamps and blondes have in common?
A: They both tend to be hot, but not too bright.

A farmer walks into his bedroom carrying a lamb under his arm. He walks over to his wife who's lying in bed. "See!" he yells, "This is the pig I have to have sex with whenever you get one of your headaches!" The wife says, "You know that's a lamb under your arm, don't you?" The farmer says, "I wasn't talking to you."

What did the psychiatrist say when a man wearing nothing but saran wrap walked in to the office? I can clearly see "you're" nuts....

A representative for a condom company is on her way to a convention. While rushing through the airport, she drops the briefcase carrying her samples of condoms all over the floor. As she is stuffing all the condoms back into her briefcase, she notices tourists giving her crazy looks. "It's ok, she says, "I am doing a huge convention."

A little kid was out trick-or-treating on Halloween dressed as a pirate. He rang a house's doorbell and the door was opened by a lady. "Oh, how cute! A little pirate! And where are your buccaneers?" she asked. The boy replied, "Under my buckin' hat."

Two lawyers walking through the woods spotted a vicious looking bear. The first lawyer immediately opened his briefcase, pulled out a pair of sneakers and started putting them on. The second lawyer looked at him and said, "You're crazy! You'll never be able to outrun that bear!" "I don't have to," the first lawyer replied. "I only have to outrun you."

A local United Way office realized that the organization had never received a donation from the town's most successful lawyer. The person in charge of contributions called him to persuade him to contribute. "Our research shows that out of a yearly income of at least $500,000, you did not give a penny to charity. Wouldn't you like to give back to the community in some way?" The lawyer mulled this over for a moment and replied, "First, did your research also show that my mother is dying after a long illness, and has medical bills that are several times her annual income?" Embarrassed, the United Way rep mumbled, "Um, no." The lawyer interrupts, "Or that my brother, a disabled veteran, is blind and confined to a wheelchair?" The stricken United Way rep began to stammer out an apology, but was interrupted again. "Or that my sister's husband died in a traffic accident," the lawyer's voice rising in indignation, "leaving her penniless with three children?!" The humiliated United Way rep, completely beaten, said simply, "I had no idea." On a roll, the lawyer cut him off once again, "So if I don't give any money to them, why should I give any to you?"

An alcoholic, a sex addict, and a pothead all die and go to Hell. Satan is waiting for them and tells all of them, "I am in a good mood today, so I am going to let each one of you pick one thing you love from Earth, and let you keep it here for 100 years, and then I will return for the goods." Satan first approaches the alcoholic, "What is it that you would like to have?" to which the alcoholic responds, "I want the finest brew, wine, and liquor you can get me." Satan brings him to a room filled with every type of beer on tap, the finest aged cellars of wine, and of course the purest grain alcohol. There is each type of liquor you could possibly think of or never afford to even taste, a never ending supply of it all. The man yells, "Woo Hoo!" in excitement, and runs into the room. Satan laughs, shuts the door, and locks it. Satan then approaches the sex addict and asks,

"What is it that you would like to have?" to which the sex addict responds, "Women! I want lots of beautiful women, one for each day of the year!" Satan brings him to a room filled with only the most gorgeous women imaginable. Some with huge breasts, some with small breasts, some with big asses, and some with small asses, some tall with never ending legs, and some short, some have tight pussies and some have shaved pussies. All of the women are hot, naked, and very horny. The sex addict immediately gets a raging hard on and runs into the room. Satan laughs, shuts the door and locks it. Satan finally approaches the pothead and asks, "What is it that you would like to have?" to which the pothead responds, "Well, that's easy! I want the best pot you got." Satan brings him to a room which is filled with the tallest, thickest, stinkiest, most dank plants growing on for acres. The sweet smell from the purest plants fills this enormous room. There were crystals growing on some buds which grew 15 feet high, just begging to be harvested. The quality of the bud would put the Cannabis Cup winners to shame, in all categories. It was beyond belief. The pothead was so awed and humbled by the sight of these beautiful plants, that he slowly walked into the room, he sat down Indian style, with his legs crossed, took slow deep breaths, closed his eyes and proceeded to meditate on this miraculous sight. Satan looked at him curiously, shut the door and locked it. 100 years pass. Satan returns to the first room, remembering the alcoholic, unlocks and opens the door. There are broken wine and liquor glass bottles shattered everywhere. The room smells like rotting animal flesh and piss. The alcoholic comes running at the door, naked, covered in his own vomit and shit, screaming "Help!, I don't want anymore. Let me out of here!" Satan laughs, shuts the door, and locks it. Satan then returns to the second room, remembering the sex addict, unlocks and opens the door. There are thousands of kids running around the room and babies crying madly making so much noise no one could hear their own screams. Hundreds of very, very old ladies now limp around with no clothes on, still very horny for the sex addict who attempts to run out the door as Satan watches. Before the sex addict can utter a word of desperation, Satan laughs, shuts the door, and locks it. Satan finally arrives at the third and final room, remembering the pothead, unlocks, and opens the door. After a quick look inside, Satan's evil grin turns to a look of confusion. Nothing had changed. The plants were untouched, just as dank as the day he left them. Even the pothead was in the same position, sitting down with his legs crossed. So Satan walks up behind the pothead, taps him on his shoulder and says, "What's wrong?" A tear rolls down the pothead's cheek as he turns to Satan and simply replies, "Got a light, man?"

You're so ugly, your husband takes you with him everywhere he goes, so he doesn't have to kiss you goodbye.

Late one night, a preacher was driving on a country road and had a wreck. A farmer stopped and said, "Sir, are you okay?" The preacher said, "Yes, I had the Lord riding with me." The farmer said, "Well, you better let him ride with me, because you're gonna kill him."

Every ten years, the monks in the monastery are allowed to break their vow of silence to speak two words. Ten years go by and it's one monk's first chance. He thinks for a second before saying, "Food bad." Ten years later, he says, "Bed hard." It's the big day, a decade later. He gives the head monk a long stare and says, "I quit." "I'm not surprised," the head monk says. "You've been complaining ever since you got here."

Q: What's Forrest Gump's password?
A: 1forrest1

How do you make five pounds of fat look good? Put a nipple on it!

The Taco Bell Chihuahua, a Doberman, and a Bulldog are in a bar having a drink, when a great looking female Collie comes up to them and says, "Whoever can say liver and cheese in a sentence can have me." So the Doberman says, "I love liver and cheese." The Collie replies, "That's not good enough." The Bulldog says, "I hate liver and cheese." She says, "That's not creative enough." Finally, the Chihuahua says, "Liver alone, cheese mine."

A string walks into a bar and orders a drink. The bartender turns to him and says, "Sorry, sir, we don't serve strings here." The next day, clinging to a thread, the string returns to that same bar and orders a drink again. The bartender, resolute, again turns and says, "I'm sorry, sir, but like I said, we don't serve strings here. I'm going to have to ask you not to return." Dejected, the string returns home. All night he tosses and turns, wriggles and writhes, and awakes the next morning not at all resembling himself. Catching a glimpse of himself in the mirror, he brightens and jets out his door to that bar. Swaggering in, he orders a drink one more time. The bartender stares at him, squinty eyed, and asks, "I'm sorry, are you a string? You look very familiar." The string locks eyes with the bartender, and states, "No, sir. I'm a frayed knot."

A neutron walks into a bar and says, "I'd like a beer. How much will that be?" The bartender responds, "For you? No charge!"

A newlywed man is going away on a business trip for 3 weeks and doesn't want his brand new bride to get lonely and mess around while he's gone. He stops by the local sex toy shop in town. He looks around, but doesn't see anything that would keep his wife occupied for 3 weeks. He asks the clerk for a recommendation. The clerk takes a black box from underneath the counter, assuring the newlywed that its contents are not for sale. He opens the box, and inside is what appears to be a normal dildo. The newlywed guy is unimpressed, but the clerk says, "Let me demonstrate." He looks at the dildo and says, "Voodoo dick, the counter!" and the dildo jumps out of the box. The clerk commands, "Voodoo dick, the box!" and the dildo hops back into the box. The newlywed man asks how much it costs, but the clerk insists it is a priceless heirloom. The newlywed man takes $500 cash out of his wallet and the clerk quickly hands over the dildo. When the man arrives home, he gives his wife the box, explains how it works, and leaves the next morning on his business trip. A few days later the wife is bored and horny, so she opens the box and skeptically says, "Voodoo dick, my pussy." After about 15 minutes, she has had several orgasms and is starting to get tired, so she tries to pull the voodoo dick out. Her husband had forgotten to tell her how to make it stop. She puts on a dress and drives to the hospital. On the way there, the voodoo dick is still going at her so the lady is speeding and swerving her car. A police officer pulls her over. The cop asks, "Lady, why are you driving so recklessly?" She explains, "Officer, there's this voodoo dick going at my pussy and I can't make it stop! I'm on the way to the hospital to have it removed!" The officer laughs and says, "Yeah right, lady. Voodoo dick, my ass."

Three men all die on Christmas Day and arrive at the pearly gates. Peter greets them and tells them that they are all evil men who should go to hell, but because it's Christmas, he'll let them into heaven if they have something representing the holiday with them. One of the guys has a Christmas ornament, and gets let in. Another guy has pine needles on his shirt, and gets let in. The third guy pulls out a pair of panties. "How do those represent Christmas?" asks Peter. "These are Carol's."

A blonde, brunette and redhead were smoking cigarettes one afternoon. The blonde had Camels, redhead had Marlboros, and the brunette had Kools. It began to pour down raining, so the redhead and brunette both pull out condoms and put them on their cigarettes. The blonde asks, "What are you doing?" and they reply, "We're saving it for later." Impressed, and in a hurry, the blonde goes to the nearest store and asks for a condom. The clerk says "What size: small, medium, or large?" She answers, "I don't know, one to fit a camel?"

Q: What's the difference between a tire and 365 used rubbers?
A: One is a Goodyear and the other is a great year.

A penguin takes his car to the shop, and the mechanic says he needs an hour to check it out. So the penguin goes across the street to the 7-Eleven to kill some time and get an ice cream. Since the penguin has no hands, the poor little guy gets the ice cream all over his beak. He returns to the mechanic and the guy tells him, "Looks like you blew a seal." "Oh no," says the penguin, "this is just a little ice cream."

Two rednecks were walking along when they saw a dog licking its balls. The first redneck said, "I wish I could do that." The other redneck said, "You dumbass, he would bite you."

Two nuns from Ireland come to tour New York City. Before they come, they hear that Americans eat dogs, so they both agree to try it when they arrive. As they're walking around New York, they hear, "Hot Dogs! Get your hot dogs!" They rush over to get one! As the first nun opens hers, her face turns white and she gasps, "What part did you get?!"

Four nuns are in line to go into heaven. God asks the first nun if she has ever sinned. She says, "Well, I've seen a penis." So God puts holy water on her eyes and lets her enter. He asks the second nun the same thing and she says, "I've held a penis," so he puts holy water on her hands and lets her enter. Then the fourth nun skips the third nun in line and God asks why she did that. The 4th nun replies, "Well, I need to gargle it before she sits in it."

Two sperms are racing to reach the ovule. After a minute, one asks the other, "Hey, how much longer until we reach the ovaries?" The other answers "Keep swimming, fool! We haven't even passed the tonsils yet!"

Yo mama is so stupid she thought fruit punch was a gay boxer.

Blonde: "You ever smelled moth balls?"
Redhead: "Yes, I think they smell good."
Blonde: "Wow, I can't believe you got your nose between those tiny legs."

Q: Why don't Mexicans like to barbecue?
A: Because the beans fall through the grill.

A teenage boy takes a quadriplegic girl on a date to dinner and the movies. At the end of the night out, he drives her back home and they start making out in his car. He tells the girl he feels uncomfortable doing this where her parents could come outside and catch them in the act. She says not to worry because she has a place they can go. So he helps her in her chair and she tells him to wheel her into the backyard. When they get in the back, she shows him a huge weeping willow tree that they can hide under and says he can do whatever he wants to her. Under the tree, she shows him two branches that can prop her up and he has his way with her. When they finish, he dresses himself and her, puts back into her chair, wheels her to the front door, and knocks. When her father sees the young man, he thanks him. The boy feels very uncomfortable because of what he just did to the man's daughter and asks, "Why are you thanking me?" "Because son," the father answers, "You are the first boy to take her out of the tree."

An elderly woman went to her local doctor's office and asked to speak with her doctor. When the receptionist asked why she was there, she replied, I'd like to have some birth control pills. Taken back, the doctor thought for a minute and then said, "Excuse me, Mrs. Glenwood, but you're 80 years old. What would you possibly need birth control pills for?" The woman replied, "They help me sleep better." The doctor considered this for a second, and continued, "How in the world do birth control pills help you sleep?" The woman said, "I put them in my granddaughter's orange juice, and I sleep better at night."

There was this homeless drunk dude laying in an alley talking out loud saying, "I wish had another drink." He then passed out. As he was saying that, a gay dude was walking by and heard him. When the gay guy came back, he fucked the homeless guy and put three dollars in his pocket. The homeless dude woke up later and found the money, ran to the liquor store, and said, "Give me the cheapest half of pint you have," and went back to his spot, drunk it and passed out again. The gay dude came back, fucked the homeless dude again, and left five dollars. He ran back to the liquor store and said, "Give me the cheapest pint you have," and went back to his spot. The gay dude came back again. Once he saw the homeless man passed out, he fucked him again and left eight dollars the homeless dude woke up and realized he had some more money. He ran back to the liquor store, and before he could say a word, the owner said, "I know, you want the cheapest pint you can get," and the homeless dude said, "No, give me the most expensive half you got. That cheap liquor is tearing my ass up."

Jack and Jill went up the hill so Jack could lick her candy. Jack got a shock, with a mouth full of cock, to find out Jill's real name was Randy.

How does a man show that he is planning for the future? He buys two cases of beer.

A man is about to enter a meeting at work when he realizes that he forgot some important paperwork. He calls home so that his wife can retrieve them. The maid answers the phone and says that his wife is busy. He demands that the maid put his wife on the phone. The maid informs the man that his wife is in bed with the gardener. The man goes nuts, and offers the maid one million dollars to shoot them both. The maid agrees and he soon hears two gunshots. The maid returns to the phone and he asks her what happened. The maid says she shot his wife in bed and the gardener ran, so she shot him by the pool. The man says, "Pool??? Is this 555-4320???"

Did you hear about the gay midget? He came out of the cupboard.

What did one lesbian vampire say to the other? Same time next month?

Have you heard about the two gay Irishmen? Mike Fitzpatrick and Patrick Fitzmike.

A guy walks into a bar with his pet monkey. He orders a drink and while he's drinking it the monkey is running wild. The monkey jumps up on the pool table and grabs the cue ball, sticks it in his mouth and swallows it whole. The bartender is livid and says to the guy, "Did you see what your monkey just did?" "No. What did that stupid monkey do this time?" says the patron. "Well, he just swallowed the cue ball off the pool table, whole" says the bartender. "Yeah, well I hope it kills him because he's been driving me nuts," says the patron. The guy finishes his drink and leaves. Two weeks later he comes back with the monkey. He orders a drink and the monkey starts running wild around the bar again. While the man is drinking his drink, the monkey finds some peanuts on the bar. He grabs one, sticks it up his butt, then pulls it out and eats it. The bartender is disgusted. "Did you see what your monkey did now?" he asks. "What now?" responds the patron. "Well, he stuck a peanut up his butt, then pulled it out and ate it" says the bartender. "Well, what do you expect?" replied the patron. "Ever since he ate that darn cue ball he measures everything first!"

A couple drives to the hospital because the wife is in labor. The doctor alerts them that she invented a machine that will transfer some of the labor pain to the father, if they'd like. The husband eagerly says, "Give it all to me!" The couple returns home with a bouncing baby boy, only to find the mailman dead on their lawn.

A limbless man sat on the side of a lake every day. He had no arms or no legs. One day he was crying when a woman was walking by and saw that he was upset, so she asked if he was okay. He replied, "No." The woman said, "Well, what's wrong?" The limbless man said, "I've never been hugged by anyone ever." So the woman, out of kindness, hugged the man. "Are you okay now?" she asked. "No," the man replied. So again the woman asked him what was wrong. He answered, "I've never been kissed before." The woman eagerly gave him a peck on the lips and asked, "Are you okay now?" The man shook his head sadly. The woman asked him what was wrong for the third time. The man said, "I've never been fucked." The woman looked at him, picks him up, throws him in the lake, and says, "Now you are!"

A blonde police officer pulls over a blonde driver and says, "You failed to stop at the red light. Let me see your driver's license." The blonde asks, "What does that look like?" The blonde cop answers, "It is rectangular and has your picture on it." The blonde looks around inside her purse and mistakes her mirror for the license. When she hands it to the blonde officer, he looks at it and replies, "Oh, I didn't know you were also an officer. You can go!"

A man walks out on his front porch one day and sees a gorilla in the tree on his front lawn. He calls animal control and about an hour later a man shows up with a ladder, a pit bull, and a shotgun. The animal control employee tells the man, "I'm here to get the gorilla out of your tree. I'm going to use this ladder to climb up the tree and shake the branch the gorilla is on to knock him to the ground. The pit bull is trained to go after anything that falls from the tree and bites their balls which calms the animal down so I can put him in the truck." The man says "Okay, I see what the ladder and the pit bull are for but what is the shotgun for?" The animal control employee says, "Oh, that's for you. In case I fall out of the tree instead of the gorilla, shoot the dog."

Did you hear about the blondes that froze to death at a drive-in movie theater? They went to see "Closed for the Winter."

The teacher asked little Johnny to use the word "definitely" in a sentence. Little Johnny replies, "Teacher, do farts have lumps in them?" The teacher says, "Of course not Johnny." To which Johnny replies, "Then I have definitely shit my pants."

Q: What do you call a bunch of white people in an elevator? A: A box of crackers.

A blonde is swimming in a river. A man walks up and asks her, "What are you doing in there?" She says, "I'm washing my clothes." The man asks, "Why don't you use a washing machine?" The blonde says, "I tried that, but I got too dizzy.

A guy is sitting at a bar, and a drunk dude walks up to him, calling his mom a whore. The first guy just ignores it and stays in his spot drinking his beer. An hour goes by and the drunk dude comes back saying, "Your mom is a whore!" The first guy looks around the bar, sees people staring and says, "Don't worry, everything is cool here," and shrugs it off. After a few more shots, the drunk dude walks up a third time and says, "Your mom... is such... a whore!" The guy finally gets mad, throws his fist on the table and says, "You know what, Dad? Go home!"

So there's a black guy, a white guy, and a Mexican. They find a genie's lamp, they rub it, and poof appears the genie! The genie goes to the black guy and asks, "What's your one wish?" The black guy goes, "I wish for me and all my people to be back in Africa, happy and everything." So poof! His wish is granted. Then, the genie goes to the Mexican and asks, "What's your one wish?" The Mexican goes, "I wish for me and all my people to be in Mexico, happy and everything." So poof! His wish is granted. Now, the genie goes over to the white guy and asks, "What's your one wish?" and the white guy asks, "You mean to tell me that all the black and Mexican people are out of America?" The genie replies, "Yes." So the white guy goes, "Then I'll have a Coke."

A man and a wife were in bed one morning when the wife said, "I had a strange dream last night. I dreamed I was at a penis auction. Long penises were going for $100 and thick penises were going for $300." The husband asked, "What would mine go for?" The wife replied, "They were giving ones like yours away for free." The husband said, "I also had a dream last night about an auction where they were selling juicy vaginas for $500 and tight vaginas for $1,000." "How about mine?" the wife asked and the husband replied, "That was where they were holding the auction."

Q: What do you call a nun in a wheelchair? A: Virgin Mobile

A young boy came home from school and told his mother, "I had a big fight with my classmate. He called me a sissy." The mother asked, "What did you do?" The boy replied, "I hit him with my purse!"

An English teacher told his students that when pronouncing a word beginning with the letter "H" they should ignore the "H" as in hour, honor, and honest. That day when leaving for class, he left a note for his assistant, "Please heat my rice for me." When the teacher returned to his office, he met an empty bowl. He asked the assistant, "Where is my food?" The assistant replied, "You said I should heat the rice for you, but you also instructed us to ignore the 'H.'"

A blind man walks into a store with his Seeing Eye dog. All of a sudden, he picks up the leash and begins swinging the dog over his head. The manager runs up to the man and asks, "What are you doing?!!" The blind man replies, "Just looking around."

A professor is lecturing a class and says, "Today's lecture will be about glucose. Glucose is sugar and can be found in lots of stuff. For example, semen, candy, etc." A blonde girl responds with, "How come you can't taste sugar in semen?" The professor says, "Well, sweetie, that's because you don't have taste buds in the back of your throat."

The following is a courtroom exchange between a defense attorney and a farmer with a bodily injury claim. It came from a Houston, Texas insurance agent.
Attorney: "At the scene of the accident, did you tell the constable you had never felt better in your life?"
Farmer: "That's right."
Attorney: "Well, then, how is it that you are now claiming you were seriously injured when my client's auto hit your wagon?"
Farmer: "When the constable arrived, he went over to my horse, which had a broken leg, and shot him. Then he went over to Rover, my dog, who was all banged up, and shot him. When he asked me how I felt, I just thought under the circumstances, it was a wise choice of words to say."

Three women were trapped on an island. They needed to get across the water to the mainland. They came across a genie who said, "I will grant you ladies three wishes." The first woman said, "Turn me into a fish" and she swam across the water to the other island. The second woman said, "Give me a boat" and she rowed to the other side. The third woman said, "Turn me into a man" and she walked across the bridge

What's the difference between a penis and a bonus? Your wife will always blow your bonus!

Two polish men walk past a police station. On the wall is a poster which says, "Two black men wanted for rape." One white man says to the other, "They always get the best jobs."

A man is telling his neighbor, "I just bought a new hearing aid. It cost me $4000, but its state of the art. It's perfect." "Really?" answers the neighbor. "What kind is it?" "12:30."

A hillbilly family's only son saves up money to go to college. After about three years, he comes back home. They are sitting around the dinner table, when the dad says, "Well son, you done gone to college, so you must be perty smart. Why don't you speak some math fer' us?" "Ok, Pa." The son then says, "Pi R squared." After a moment, the dad says, "Why son, they ain't teached ya nothin'! Pie are round, cornbread are square."

Yo mamma just like a freezer: she lets everyone put their meat in her.

Q: What do you call an ocean voyage where everyone stays in the closet?
A: A Tom Cruise.

A man walks into a bar and asks the bartender, "If I show you a really good trick, will you give me a free drink?" The bartender considers it, and then agrees. The man reaches into his pocket and pulls out a tiny rat. He reaches into his other pocket and pulls out a tiny piano. The rat stretches, cracks his knuckles, and proceeds to play the blues. The bartender pours the man a drink on the house and he puts the rat and piano away. After the man finished his drink, he asked the bartender, "If I show you an even better trick, will you give me free drinks for the rest of the evening?" The bartender agrees, thinking that no trick could possibly be better than the first. The man reaches into his pockets again and pulls out the tiny rat and tiny piano. The rat stretches, cracks his knuckles, and proceeds to play the blues. The man reaches into a third pocket and pulls out a small bullfrog, which begins to sing along with the rat's music. While the man is enjoying his beverages, a stranger confronts him and offers him $100,000.00 for the bullfrog. "Sorry," the man replies, "he's not for sale." The stranger increases the offer to $250,000.00 cash up front. "No," he insists, "he's not for sale." The stranger again increases the offer, this time to $500,000.00 cash. The man finally agrees, and turns the frog over to the stranger in exchange for the money. "Are you insane?" the bartender demanded. "That frog could have been worth millions to you, and you let him go for a mere $500,000!" "Don't worry about it," the man answered. "The frog was nothing special. You see, the rat's a ventriloquist."

I've spent the last two years looking for my wife's killer, but nobody will do it.

A husband says to his wife, "My Olympic condoms have arrived. I think I'll wear gold tonight." The wife replied, "Why not wear silver and come second for a change?"

Patient: "I get a terrible pain in my eye when I drink a cup of coffee."
Doctor: "Try taking the spoon out."

A blonde is walking down the street and a car pulled up next to her. The man in the car says to her, "What do you have in the bag?" The blonde replies: "I have chickens!" The man thinks for a moment and says, "If I can guess how many chickens you have in the bag, can I have one?" The blonde thinks that it sounds fair and replies, "Okay, but I'll make the bet even better! If you can guess exactly how many chickens I have in the bag I will give you BOTH of them!"

A woman constantly keeps sneezing and goes to see the doctor. She tells him, "Doctor, I constantly keep sneezing, and every time I sneeze, I have an orgasm." The doctor asks, "What are you doing for it?" The woman replies, "Sniffing pepper."

There were five people aboard an airplane having engine trouble getting ready to crash; however, there were only four parachutes. Everyone wondered what should be done to determine who should get the parachutes. One person said that he was the smartest thing that hit the face of the Earth, and that he was too smart to die. So, he took one of the parachutes and jumped out of the aircraft. The second person said that she was too important to die, she had children and a family to take care of, and they depended on her to care for them. So, she took one of the parachutes and jumped out of the aircraft. The third person said that he was too important to die because his family depended on him for survival. He was the head of household and the sole bread winner. So, he took one of the parachutes and jumped out of the aircraft. Finally, there were only two people left, and one parachute. One person was a 12 year old boy, and the other was a 65 year old man. The old man said, "Well son, I have lived a good life, and you are too young to die, you have a long life ahead of you. So, you take the last parachute. The boy asked, "Why, Sir?" The old man said, "Well, there is only one parachute left." The little lad said, "Sir there are really two parachutes left." The old gentlemen asked, excitedly, "Yeah? How?" "Well," replied the boy, "you know that guy who thought he was the smartest and greatest thing that hit the face of the Earth? He grabbed my backpack."

If you want to know who is really man's best friend, put your dog and your wife in the trunk of your car, come back an hour later, open the trunk, and see which one is happy to see you.

A girl realized that she had grown hair between her legs. She got worried and asked her mom about that hair. Her mom said, "Don't worry. That part where the hair has grown is called a Monkey. Be proud that your monkey has grown hair." At dinner, the girl told her sister, "My monkey has grown hair." Her sister replied, "That's nothing. Mine is already eating bananas."

Seven year old Lebron was in English class, when his teacher asked him to use dictate in a sentence. So he says, "Lass night I heard Daddy askin' Momma, 'how do my dictate?'"

A Scotsman, who was driving home one night, ran into a car driven by an Englishman. The Scotsman got out of the car to apologize and offered the Englishman a drink from a bottle of whisky. The Englishman was glad to have a drink. "Go on," said the Scot, "Have another drink." The Englishman drank gratefully. "But don't you want one, too?" he asked the Scotsman. "Perhaps," replied the Scotsman, "after the police have gone."

An old man and his wife went to the doctor for a check-up. While the man is with the doctor, the doctor asks him, "So how has life been treating you?" The old man replies, "The Lord's been good to me. Every night when I go to the bathroom, he turns the light on and when I'm finished, he turns the light off." While the old woman is with the doctor, the doctor told her what her husband said. She replied, "Damn it! The old fart's been pissing in the ice box again!"

A man and a woman have just had their 50th wedding anniversary. The husband turns to his wife and asks, "What do you want to do to celebrate our anniversary dear?" She replies, "Let's run upstairs and make love." He turns to her and says, "Well make up your mind, we can't do both!"

Worried about their less than exciting sex life, a young wife sends her husband to a therapist who winds up treating him with self-hypnosis. To her joy, everything gets much better. However, she can't help but notice that each night, just before their lovemaking, the husband dashes out to the bathroom for several minutes. This torments her until finally, one night, she follows him. There, in front of the mirror, she finds him applying this therapeutic technique, "She's not my wife. She's not my wife. She's not my wife."

How much coke has Charlie Sheen snorted? Enough to kill two and a half men.

A wife says, "Hey! Look at that funny guy who has been drinking a lot." The husband responds, "Who is he?" The wife answers, "Well, five years ago, he was my boyfriend and I denied him for marriage." "Oh my God! He's still celebrating his freedom!" says the husband.

A 92 year old man is walking through a park and sees a talking frog. He picks up the frog and the frogs says, "If you kiss me, I will turn into a beautiful princess and be yours for a week." The old man puts the frog in his pocket. The frog screams, "Hey if you kiss me, I will turn into a beautiful princess and make love to you for a whole month." The old man looks at the frog and says, "At my age I'd rather have a talking frog."

There are three women. One is dating, one is engaged, and one is married. They decide to get kinky with their men and really pull out all the stops to make it extra special. The woman who is dating says, "Okay, so I bought black leather, red lipstick, fishnet stockings, and really got crazy. He loved it so much he thinks he's in love." The woman who is engaged says, "I showed up to his work after hours wearing only a red coat. Let's just say he wants to move the wedding date up!" The woman who is married says, "Okay, I really went all out. I got a babysitter for the kids, and bought a black mask and a whip. My husband gets home, goes straight to the fridge, and grabs a beer. Then he plops down on the couch and says, 'Hey Batman! Where the fuck is dinner?!?'"

I met a one-legged woman outside of a club the other day. She was a bouncer.

Two guys are at a bar on the roof of a hotel. One guy says to the other guy, "I'll bet you a beer that I can jump off this building, let this wind take me all the way around this building, and I'll land back up here." The other guy says, "You're on." The first guy jumps and, sure enough, he goes around the building and lands back on the roof. "You owe me a beer," he says. He goes on to perform the trick several more times, collecting free beers, until the second guy decides he's going to try it too. He stands on the edge, looking forward to a free beer from the first man, and jumps off, dying when he slams into the pavement below. The bartender says to the first man, "You sure are an asshole when you're drunk, Superman."

As a group of soldiers stood in formation at an Army Base, the Drill Sergeant said, "All right! All you idiots fall out." As the rest of the squad wandered away, one soldier remained at attention. The Drill Instructor walked over until he was eye to eye with him, and then raised a single eyebrow. The soldier smiled and said, "Sure was a lot of 'em, huh, sir?"

An elephant and a camel are talking. The elephant asks, "Why do you have boobs on your back?" The camel replies, "Ha! That's a funny question coming from an animal with a penis hanging from his face."

A man goes to a pet shop and buys a talking parrot. He takes the parrot home and tries to teach the parrot how to say a few things, but instead, the parrot just swears at him.

After a few hours of trying to teach the bird, the man finally says, "If you don't stop swearing, I'm going to put you in the freezer as punishment." The parrot continues, so finally the man puts the bird in the freezer. About an hour later, the parrot asks the man to please open the door. As the man takes the shivering bird out of the freezer, it says, "I promise to never swear again. Just tell me what that turkey did!"

A hippie backpacker from the Swiss Alps was tramping across a farmer's field when it got dark. He asked the farmer if he could spend the night. The farmer agreed but said he would have to sleep in bed with his 18 year old daughter. The farmer told him, "If I catch you molesting my daughter I'll shoot you!" That night the hippie and the farmer's daughter got it on and had a great time. The farmer could hear the goings on from the next room. In the morning he opened the door and asked the hippie, "Did you have sex with my daughter?" The hippie was a Jesus freak so he decided to be honest: "Yes, I did. Please forgive me." The farmer took the hippie out back of the house and pointed a shotgun at him. "Ya got any last words, bub?" he asked. The Swiss hippie said, "Yodelayheehoo!" Then the farmer shot him. When the Sheriff arrived, he asked the farmer why he shot the man just for having sex with his daughter. The farmer replied, "Well, I didn't really have a problem with him screwing Bonnie. I was just gonna scare him a little, but when he said, 'Yer 'ol lady too!' that's when I blew his head off."

A carpet layer had just finished installing carpet for a lady. He stepped out for a smoke, only to realize he'd lost his cigarettes. In the middle the room, under the carpet, was a bump. "No sense pulling up the entire floor for one pack smokes," he said to himself. He proceeded to get out his hammer and flattened the hump. As he was cleaning up, the lady came in. "Here," she said, handing him his cigarette pack. "I found them in the hallway. Now, if only I could find my sweet little hamster."

Two nuns were riding their bicycles down the street. The first nun says, "I've never came this way before." The second nun says, "Yeah, it's the cobblestones!"

Printed in Great Britain
by Amazon